Christmas, 1970.
We hope this book will
be a blessing to you.
Love
Ermina, Joe
and family

PROPHETIC TRUTH
UNFOLDING
TODAY

PROPHETIC TRUTH
UNFOLDING
TODAY

EDITED BY

Charles Lee Feinberg

Messages delivered at the Congress on Prophecy convened by the American Board of Mission to the Jews, Inc., in the metropolitan New York area.

Fleming H. Revell Company
Old Tappan, New Jersey

Scripture quotations not otherwise identified are from the King James Version of the Bible.

Scripture quotations identified as ASV are from the American Standard Version of the Bible. (In these passages, the name "the Lord" has been substituted for "Jehovah.")

To

The Reverend Daniel Fuchs, D.D.
The Reverend Emil Daniel Gruen, D.D.
The Reverend Harold Bruce Pretlove

SERVANTS OF CHRIST

LEADERS OF MEN

LOVERS OF ISRAEL

this volume is respectfully and gratefully dedicated

Contributors

E. Schuyler English, Litt.D.
Chairman, Scofield Editorial Committee; President, Pilgrim Fellowship

Charles Lee Feinberg, Th.D., Ph.D.
Dean, Professor of Semitics and Old Testament; Talbot Theological Seminary

Daniel Fuchs, D.D.
Missionary Secretary, American Board of Missions to the Jews, Inc.

Frank E. Gaebelein, Litt.D., LL.D., D.D.
Headmaster Emeritus, The Stony Brook School

Allan A. MacRae, A.M., Ph.D.
President, Faith Theological Seminary

Clarence E. Mason, Jr., Th.M., D.D.
Dean, Philadelphia College of Bible

Stephen F. Olford, D.D., Litt.D.
Pastor, Calvary Baptist Church, New York City

John F. Walvoord, A.M., Th.D.
President, Dallas Theological Seminary

Table of Contents

Foreword

The Fifth Congress on Prophecy, convened under God's leading by the American Board of Missions to the Jews in the greater New York area in May of 1967, met at a crisis hour. Daily the news media—newspapers, radio, and television—headlined the conflict in the world. The Israel-Arab confrontation was moving toward a head-on collision. The nations of the world were jockeying for position and power. In the Far East, China was perfecting her hydrogen bomb, thus placing in the hands of a government which has no concern for human lives and values an instrument that can destroy the whole world. In Christendom there was an ever-increasing crescendo of apostasy: the denial of God's existence, of the inerrancy of His Word, of the basic mission of the church, even of our very Lord Jesus Christ and His atoning work upon Calvary. It was to these problems that the Congress addressed itself, not using headlines to interpret the Bible but using the Bible to explain the headlines. How well this task was carried out can be seen in the contents of this book.

The Congress was privileged to have as its speakers men who are mighty in the Word, teachers of prophetic truth of world renown. Six of them were members of the committee which has given to the world the *New Scofield Reference Bible*. It was of the Lord's leading that the Congress should follow by a few weeks the publication of this revised edition of the Bible, which has been such a useful tool in the hands of Christian workers and Bible students. The truths proclaimed at the Congress have been clearly set forth in the study helps of this Bible since its first publication.

The Congress did not overlook the application of the great truths proclaimed to the need around us. We met in an area which contains more than two million Jews, as well as seven million Gentiles. Missionary hours were held daily, and the proclamation of the gospel to the Jew and Gentile alike was an important part

of our study as well as our prayers. Hearts were blessed as our
missionaries spoke of victories won in lives surrendered to Jesus
Christ, Israel's Messiah and the world's Redeemer. If the coming
of our Lord is nigh, then the challenge of the hour is great; we
must redeem the time that is left to us.

We recognize with gratefulness the gracious welcome of the
three great churches in which the Congress met: the Calvary Baptist Church of New York City, the Brookdale Baptist Church of
Bloomfield, New Jersey, and the Franklin Avenue Baptist Church
of Malverne, New York.

We are also very grateful to Dr. Charles Lee Feinberg for his
gracious willingness to accept the responsibility of the editorship
of this book. It has been well said that to get a task done right,
give it to a busy man to do.

To all who have had a part in this book: To the speakers for
their permission to publish the messages, to Dr. Feinberg for his
fine work of editing, and to the staff of the Fleming H. Revell
Company for their interest and cooperation in the producing of
this volume, go our heartfelt thanks. Above all our praise goes to
our God who permitted us to gather together in such a Congress
on Prophecy and then to enlarge the outreach of the ministry and
blessings of that gathering through the publishing of this book.
May His blessings be upon this effort; may the lives of many of
His children be strengthened hereby, and may the soon coming of
our Lord Jesus Christ become more wonderful and real to all who
read this book.

> *Emil D. Gruen*
> *Conference Secretary,*
> *American Board of Missions*
> *to the Jews, Inc.*

Preface

It was in November 1942 that the First Congress on Prophecy met at Calvary Baptist Church of New York City. The hour was dark, and the powers of evil were rampant throughout a war-mad world. Much hung in the balance, and only God's Word was the sufficient support at that stage of world history. Nearly twenty-five years later, in May, 1967, at the same church a roster of Bible teachers again enunciated the truths so warmly presented a quarter of a century before by mighty voices in the church, a number of them now in the presence of the Lord. And the hour was again freighted with anxiety as Israel's enemies fulminated against her with the declared object of her extinction. It is now a matter of history how God enabled Israel to withstand that devastating threat to her survival.

It is often asked why there is so much emphasis on prophecy in these days. Is it not overdone? Would it not be better if it were softened down a bit? But prophecy today is not being exploited for sensational reasons; this century is preeminently the century of prophetic fulfillment. Apart from the first century A.D., which saw the life, ministry, atoning work, and resurrection of the Lord Jesus Christ, the twentieth century has already witnessed more fulfillment of prophecy than all the other centuries of man's existence on earth. Basis enough, we should think, for sustained interest and attention to prophetic themes.

It will be seen that the participants in the conference included six of the committee who revised the time-honored *Scofield Reference Bible*, the present edition appearing on April 13, 1967. This is not to be taken to mean that this volume is a reflection, either officially or otherwise, of viewpoints held by the Oxford University Press.

Thanks are here extended to the beloved pastor of the Calvary Baptist Church of New York City, the Rev. Dr. Stephen F. Olford, who has graciously favored us with two of his messages at

the conference; to my esteemed colleagues in the Revision Committee of the *New Scofield Reference Bible* and co-laborers in the
conference, who out of exceedingly busy lives and ministries yet
found time to submit their manuscripts for this volume; to the
Rev. Dr. Daniel Fuchs for his contribution of a chapter relating
the new revision to the task of Jewish Missions; to the Rev. Dr.
Emil D. Gruen, Conference Secretary of the American Board of
Missions to the Jews, Inc., truly the conference director par excel-
lence, who acted as host to the sessions, looked after the
many needs of the speakers, and also assisted in gathering the
manuscripts for this book; and finally, to the editorial staff of
Fleming H. Revell Company for their kind help in seeing the work
through the press.

This work is commended to the blessing of God that it may be
used to glorify Christ, to magnify the Word of God, to quicken
saints to the task of preaching Christ to Jews and Gentiles, and to
the garnering of souls from among the lost into whose hands these
pages may come.

> *Charles Lee Feinberg*
> *Talbot Theological Seminary*
> *La Mirada, California*

I

The Church on Earth

E. Schuyler English

I had a friend who lived and died by one book, the Bible. But he read other literature also. Included in these writings were the works of Shakespeare, which he knew almost as well as he did the Scriptures. On one occasion my friend told me that if he were to visit the Shakespearean theater in Stratford-on-Avon, and were he permitted to go behind the curtain about fifteen minutes before the play began, he could discern which of Shakespeare's plays was to be enacted, simply by observation. I asked him how he could do this. As nearly as I can recall what he said, this was his reply:

Let us suppose that I go behind the curtain and observe scene-shifters setting the stage for the play. The backdrop represents a medieval castle with gray stone walls. Immediately I would eliminate *Macbeth,* because its opening scene is a desert place. *Romeo and Juliet* begins in a public square, so that is not the play. Neither can it be *The Merchant of Venice* or *Othello,* since nothing of Venice is suggested on the backdrop. There is no ship, so *The Tempest* must be excluded. The opening scene of *Antony and Cleopatra* is a palace room, not a wall. Now only a few great Shakespearean plays are left.

I turn and see some of the actors getting ready to go on stage. None of them wears a Roman toga, so I know that *Julius Caesar* will not be played tonight. But then I observe a couple dressed in royal apparel. Another actor appears in a costume that simulates a ghost. I am about to make my decision when it is clinched for me, for leaning against a wall adjacent to the stage entrance are some shields embossed with the arms of Denmark. I know what I am to see this evening—*Hamlet.*

Great events are to come on the stage of world history. Many people wonder what lies ahead. They see before them a huge curtain that veils the coming drama. They know nothing of what the Bible tells about the future and consequently cannot see the shifting of the scenes or the actors preparing to play their parts in the divine program. But he who is well acquainted with the prophetic Scriptures can step behind the curtain of ignorance and time, and discern preparations that are already under way pointing to predicted events. He knows the plot—God's plan for the ages. He even knows some of the lines that the actors will speak. And he sees in today's news tendencies that foreshadow the predicted drama of tomorrow.

In the prophetic Scriptures there are themes that are awesome and dramatic—beasts rise out of the earth and the sea, trumpets sound, and stars fall from the heavens. Sometimes equally important prophecies are less vivid. One of these is the place and part of the church in prophecy. Yet here also there is drama; for what could be more phenomenal than a multitude caught up into heaven without dying?

The Church Defined

It is absurd to talk about a subject unless its terms are understood. Therefore, before considering the church's place in the prophetic program, the church must be defined.

The word "church" is a translation of a Greek noun, *ekklēsia*, whose literal meaning is "a calling out." It was used in olden times to denote an assembly of people called to a public meeting. In the Septuagint, an early Greek translation of the Old Testament, the word is employed more than seventy times. I should like to emphasize, however, that this fact is not proof that the church, as it is known today, existed in Old Testament times. The church did not come into existence until the Day of Pentecost. This statement can be substantiated readily.

When Simon Peter made his firm confession as to the Deity of Christ, "Thou art the Christ, the Son of the living God," as recorded in Matthew 16:16, the Lord Jesus replied: "Blessed art thou, Simon Barjona; for flesh and blood hath not revealed it unto thee, but my Father who is in heaven. And I say unto thee, that thou art Peter, and upon this rock I will build my church; and the gates of Hades shall not prevail against it." Observe that our Lord said "I *will* build my church"—not "I *have* built my church," nor "I shall continue my church," nor "I shall restore my church," nor "I shall renew my church," nor "I shall refurbish my church"; but "I will build my church." The church was not established prior to this time. The church was something that would be built in the future.

There are four conceptions of what the church is. First and primarily, the word "church" relates to the body of believers in Christ whose entity began on the Day of Pentecost and has become worldwide in its composition. It is united with Him and held together by baptism with the Holy Spirit. It is called not only "the church," but also "the body of Christ" (I CORINTHIANS 12:13) and "the bride of Christ" (compare REVELATION 19:7). This mystical body of Christ, formed of genuine believers only, is the true church—a new thing in which, inconceivable in Old Testament times, Jews and Gentiles are made one in Christ Jesus.

Second, there is the visible church, which is composed of all who profess to bear Christ's name, unbelievers as well as believers, whatever their differences in doctrine and form of worship. This visible church comprises what is sometimes referred to as Christendom.

Third, local assemblies are designated as churches. For example, in the New Testament the church at Corinth is mentioned, and the church in Smyrna.

And fourth, an organization or fellowship of an indeterminate number of local churches is identified as a church, e.g., the Baptist Church, the Presbyterian Church, etc. "The churches of Galatia" (GALATIANS 1:2) are sometimes spoken of as "the Galatian church."

The Course of the Church Age

Of the Pharisees our Lord asked a question: "When the Son of man cometh, shall he find faith [literally, *the faith*] on the earth?" (LUKE 18:8). Neither they nor He answered the question on that occasion. Elsewhere in the New Testament, however, the answer is made clear.

In Matthew 13 the mystery parables are recorded. They reveal a great deal about the course of the church age. In these parables something entirely new is presented. Concerning them it is written: "All these things spake Jesus unto the multitude in parables . . . that it might be fulfilled which was spoken by the prophet, saying, I will open my mouth in parables; I will utter things which have been kept secret from the foundation of the world" (vv. 34-35).

The parables of Matthew 13 relate to the kingdom of heaven, or the kingdom of the heavens. They are generally introduced by the clause, "the kingdom of heaven is like. . . ." What is this kingdom of the heavens? Is it the church?

First, observe what the kingdom of the heavens is not. It is not heaven; for every scene in the parables is earthly and, furthermore, the fruit of the good seed and the bad seed is mixed. Neither is it the Messianic kingdom promised to David and his seed; for the Messianic kingdom was made known in Old Testament times, whereas here our Lord was speaking of things that had been kept secret since the foundation of the world. Nor could this kingdom of the heavens allude specifically to the true church, which is called the body of Christ, the bride of Christ, the habitation of God, a temple and a house, but never the kingdom of the heavens.

The kingdom of the heavens is something new. The expression, as used in Matthew, denotes *Christendom*—that part of the world that, since the first century, has recognized the first advent of the Messiah, Christ, and bears His name, though not always in faith. The kingdom of the heavens of Matthew's mystery parables is the visible church, composed of believers and unbelievers. So then our Lord revealed, in these seven parables, something that had been kept secret in the counsels of the Godhead throughout the ages.

The first parable of Matthew 13 is well known. It is the parable of the sower sowing seed, some of which fell by the wayside and was devoured by the fowls; some fell upon stony places and its vegetation was scorched by the sun, because the ground was shallow; other seed fell among thorns and its fruition was choked; whereas still other fell into good ground and brought forth fruit—some a hundredfold, some sixtyfold, and some thirtyfold (vv. 3-13, 18-23).

Christ Himself interpreted the parable. The seed is the Word of God. It is sown by the Son of God and falls upon men's hearts, that are likened to shallow ground, stony places, thorny ground, and good ground. The wicked one, Satan, catches away the first; trials stifle the growth of the second; the fondness for this world chokes the Word of the third, and there is no fruit. But the Word that falls into good ground, that is, receptive hearts, brings forth much fruit. Only one-fourth of the seed sown is fruitful. The other three-fourths brings no response of genuine faith.

The second parable of the chapter is the familiar story of the wheat and the tares. A man sows seed in his field. But during the night his enemy comes and sows tares. The fruit of the good seed comes forth. It is wheat. But at the same time the fruit of the enemy's seed appears. It is tares, that is, weeds. When the sower's servants ask him whether they should gather the weeds, his reply is in the negative lest, while taking up the weeds, they might take the wheat also. Both are to be left to grow together until the harvest, when the weeds are to be burned and the wheat placed in the barn (vv. 24-30, 36-43).

Here, in His interpretation, the Lord Jesus speaks of the good seed as the children of the kingdom and the bad seed as the children of the devil. The field in which the seed is sown is the world. The meaning is obvious: in this age the children of the kingdom and the children of Satan live side by side until the end of the age.

Two other companion parables in Matthew 13 suffice to underscore the mixed membership of the church in this present age.

First is the parable of a single grain of mustard seed that was sown in a field, and which, when it grew, became a tree in whose branches birds of the air lodged (vv. 31-32). As the field symbolizes the world in our Lord's interpretation of the parable of the wheat and the tares, so it does here. A mustard seed is "the least of all seeds," which normally grows into a plant or bush. But here it develops abnormally into a tree with branches in which the birds find a resting place. In the parable of the sower the birds were interpreted by Christ as being the agents of the wicked one, and in Revelation 18:2 the birds are said to be "unclean and hateful." The parable of the mustard seed substantiates what has already been shown: the Gospel seed has developed into a monstrous structure, the visible church, which possesses the life of the seed but also shelters the unconverted, the progeny of the devil.

Then there is the parable of the leaven: "The kingdom of the heavens is like unto leaven, which a woman took and hid in three measures of meal, till the whole was leavened" (v. 33). The general interpretation of this parable, even by the so-called "prince of commentators," John Peter Lange, is this: "The woman, the Church; the leaven, the Gospel; the three measures of meal, humanity; result—the life from God in its progressive victory over the natural life of the world." But I do not think this interpretation is valid.

Ask almost any orthodox Jew what leaven stands for. He will say not that it is something good but that it is something evil. The feast of unleavened bread was eaten to typify the purging of sin from the worshiper's life. Furthermore, when our Lord told His disciples to beware of the leaven of the Pharisees and of the Sadducees, He was warning His followers against the doctrine of the Pharisees and Sadducees, which was false doctrine (MATTHEW 16:11-12). And Paul wrote to the church at Corinth: "Purge out therefore the old leaven, that ye may be a new lump, as ye are unleavened" I CORINTHIANS 5:6-7).

Meal, on the other hand, is a symbol of good. It comes from wheat, not tares. When Abraham wanted to find favor in the Lord's sight, he told Sarah: "Make ready quickly three measures of fine meal, knead it, and make cakes upon the hearth" (GENESIS 18:6).

The meaning of the parable is this: Into the fruit of the seed sown by Christ, false doctrine has been implanted until it permeates all of it. The meal and the leaven are mixed. So in Christendom throughout this age, the tares grow with the wheat, the birds of the air rest in the branches of the tree, the leaven pervades the meal.

It is at the end of the age that the tares will be separated from the wheat, and not until then.

When Christ comes again, will He find the faith on the earth? Yes, some will have faith. There has always been a remnant of believers. Cain rejected God, but Abel believed and obeyed God. Elijah thought that he alone of God's people was left, but God told him that there were still seven thousand who had not bowed their knees to Baal. During disobedience in Israel, even at the height of the nation's apostasy, there was a remnant that believed and obeyed God. And so in this age. Only one-fourth of the seed sown is fruitful; but that seed, the true church, is a constant remnant—constant not because of its own faithfulness, but because of the faithfulness of the Holy Spirit who preserves the church.

The relationship between the Lord Jesus Christ and His blood-purchased people is aptly symbolized in Scripture: Christ is the Head, the church is His body; Christ is the Bridegroom, the church His bride; Christ is the Vine, the church its branches. What closer relationship could there be than members of a body one to another, and all to the head? What sweeter union could exist than a bride to her bridegroom? What could symbolize the flow of life better than the vine to its branches? To believers Christ is all and in all. His love flows out to them day by day, hour by hour; and their love for Him grows warmer as they know Him better. He bestows wisdom, strength, and grace upon grace. He guards His own, and encourages and comforts them. Sometimes He chastens them for their own good. He loves them with an unending love. He longs for the day when, in the Father's good pleasure, He can take His church to Himself. He abides with us now by His Spirit. One day we shall be in His very presence forevermore. When He comes, He will find the faith in His church.

Blessed be the God and Father of our Lord Jesus Christ, which [who] according to his abundant mercy hath begotten us again unto a living hope by the resurrection of Jesus Christ from the dead, to an inheritance incorruptible, and undefiled, and that fadeth not away, reserved in heaven for you, who are kept by the power of God through faith unto salvation ready to be revealed in the last time (I PETER 1:3-5).

The Last Days

However, as the age approaches its end, departure from the faith will increase.

In writing to his young friend Timothy, the Apostle Paul says: "Now the Spirit speaketh expressly that in the latter times some shall depart from the faith, giving heed to seducing spirits and doctrines of demons, speaking lies in hyprocrisy, having their conscience seared with a hot iron" (I TIMOTHY 4:1-2). And in the very last writing from his pen, the Apostle declares:

This know also, that in the last days perilous times shall come. For men shall be lovers of their own selves, covetous, boasters, proud, blasphemers, disobedient to parents, unthankful, unholy, without natural affection, truce-breakers, false accusers, incontinent, fierce, despisers of those that are good, traitors, heady, high-minded, lovers of pleasures more than lovers of God; having a form of godliness, but denying the power thereof: from such turn away" (II TIMOTHY 3:1-5).

Do you find anything that has a familiar sound in the descriptions, characteristics, and activities of those who profess to have faith and show a form of godliness while denying the power of God? And of those who are unholy and despise righteousness? Or have you been neglecting newspapers and newsmagazines these past several years?

The Apostle Peter, reminding his readers that in Old Testament times there were false prophets, warns them: "There shall be false teachers among you, who privily shall bring damnable heresies, even denying the Lord that bought them, and bring upon themselves swift destruction. And many shall follow their pernicious ways" (II PETER 2:1-2). It is false teachers such as these who will come in the last days, "scoffers, walking after their own lusts, and saying, Where is the promise of his [the Lord's] coming? for since the fathers fell asleep, all things continue as they were from the beginning of the creation" (II PETER 3:3-4).

The last days are already here, dear friends. But we are not in darkness that the day of the Lord's coming should overtake us as a thief. Through reading the Scriptures we have been permitted to step behind the curtain of the future to discover ahead of time how the drama begins and unfolds. The future of the church—Christ's mystical body, the true church; and that part of the visible church that is unregenerate—is clearly revealed. In the visible church apostasy is accelerating. Denial of the Lord and departure from the faith are more pronounced year after year.

The true church, the body of believers that has guarded and obeyed God's Word and has not denied the name that is above every name, watches and waits for Christ, longing for the rapture-shout that will call the church into His presence. Although no prophetic event requires fulfillment before the Lord comes for His church, certain phenomena must take place before He comes to reign. The shadows of war, disaster, hatred, betrayal, and apostasy hover over the world today.

"Ye therefore, beloved, seeing ye know these things before, beware lest ye also, being led away with the error of the wicked, fall from your own steadfastness. But grow in grace, and in the knowledge of our Lord and Saviour Jesus Christ. To him be glory both now and for ever. Amen" (II PETER 3:17-18).

II

The Church at the Tribunal

E. Schuyler English

If a poll were taken in America asking what the Bible teaches concerning judgment, I have no doubt what the answer would be. The unregenerate would say something like this: "Sometime, I don't know when, perhaps a judgment day might come. Those who are bad—murderers, wife-beaters, habitual thieves, drunkards, or perhaps adulterers—will be sent to hell, if there is a hell. Sometimes I think we already have our hell right here. Others, in fact most of us, are good, and kind, and charitable, and sympathetic. If there is a heaven, we'll go there."

Nothing could be further from the truth.

Even among genuine believers in Christ there is a shocking illiteracy concerning the Bible, so that probably very many of them would respond to the question about judgment in this way: "Someday we're all going to stand before God's judgment throne. Those who have received Christ as their Saviour will go to heaven. Others, who have rejected Christ, will be lost."

This answer is closer to the truth than the first reply, yet it is not accurate. What, then, does the Bible teach about judgment?

Major Judgments in the Bible

There are seven significant judgments mentioned in the Scriptures. One of the judgments is past—the judgment of sin; one is present—the believer's self-judgment; and five are future—the judgment of the believer's works, the judgment of Israel, the judgment of the nations, the judgment of the wicked angels, and the judgment of the great white throne. Consequently, when one runs across the words "judgment" or "condemnation" (for the latter is frequently rendered from the same Greek word as the former), there are five questions that he should ask himself, namely: (1) When does this judgment take place? (2) Where does it take place? (3) Who is the judge? (4) Who or what is being judged in this instance? And (5), What is the result of the judgment? With these questions in mind, an examination of the Bible's seven major judgments is in order.

1. *The judgment of sin.* This judgment is recorded in the four Gospels. The time was a little more than nineteen centuries ago. The place was Calvary. The judge was God the Father. It was sin that was judged. But that judgment fell upon a person, the God-Man, our Lord Jesus Christ who, though He Himself knew no sin, was made sin for us on the Cross, that we might be made the righteousness of God in Him (II CORINTHIANS 5:21). The result of the judgment is that all who put their trust in Him as the Son of God and their personal Lord and Saviour will not come into judgment but have passed from death (spiritual death) to life (eternal life) (JOHN 5:24). And "there is therefore now no condemnation [judgment] to them which are in Christ Jesus" (ROMANS 8:1). The true church will never be judged on the sin question. That judgment has been borne already by another. For believers who do sin there may be discipline and chastening in this life. Such sins need to be confessed and put under the blood of Christ. But salvation is assured for every member of the household of faith, every believer in the Lord Jesus Christ.

2. *Self-judgment.* The Scripture that tells of this judgment is I Corinthians 11:31: "For if we judge ourselves, we should not be judged." The time is now. The place is here on earth. The judge is the believer himself. The judgment is upon the believer's conduct in relation to God and his fellowmen. The result of the judgment is whether or not the believer must undergo disciplinary judgment from God in this present life, and whether he will receive or lose rewards when he stands before the judgment seat of Christ (II CORINTHIANS 5:10).

3. *The judgment of believers' works.* This judgment is recorded most fully in I Corinthians 3:9-15. The time is future, immediately after the church is caught up to meet the Lord in the air. The place? Some say that it is in the air, that is, in the heavens. It is my thought that it will be in heaven itself. The judge is the Lord Jesus; "for we shall all stand before the judgment seat of Christ" (ROMANS 14:10). That which will be judged is the works of the believer, according to what he has done, whether it is good or bad (II CORINTHIANS 5:10). The result of the judgment

will be reward or lack of reward when his work is made manifest.

4. *The judgment of Israel.* This judgment is written in Ezekiel 20:33-44. The time is in the future, at the beginning of the millennium. The place is on earth. The judge is Christ. That which will be judged is Israel's obedience or lack of it. The result of the judgment will be that those who have rebelled against God will be purged and will not enter the land of Israel. But those who hearken to Him in that day will enter the land of kingdom blessing.

5. *The judgment of the nations.* The prediction concerning this judgment is written in Matthew 25:31-46. The time is future, at the beginning of the millennial reign of Christ. The place is on earth. The judge is Christ. That which will be judged is the treatment, by individual Gentiles rather than the nations as a whole, of Christ's brethren, the Jews. The result of the judgment is that the "sheep," those who have a heart for the Jews, will enter the land of blessing, whereas the "goats," those who despise and persecute the Jewish people, will be condemned to "everlasting fire, prepared for the devil and his angels."

6. *The judgment of the wicked angels.* This judgment is announced in Jude 6. The time is future, after the millennial reign of Christ. The place is somewhere in the heavens, probably heaven itself. The judge is God the Son, inasmuch as He Himself declared: "For the Father judgeth no man, but hath committed all judgment unto the Son; that all men should honor the Son, even as they honor the Father" (JOHN 5:22-23). Those who are judged are the wicked angels. Satan is one of them, their king. It is true that Satan was defeated at Calvary. It is equally true that our Lord said that "now shall the prince of this world be cast out" (JOHN 12:31), and "the prince of this world is judged" (JOHN 16:11). However, Satan's judgment will be culminated at the end of the millennium. Like the angels who kept not their first estate, the devil too has been reserved "unto the judgment of the great day." The result of the judgment will be that Satan and his hosts will be committed to the place prepared for them, the lake of everlasting fire where they will "be tormented day and night forever and ever" (MATTHEW 25:41; REVELATION 20:10).

7. *The judgment of the great white throne.* This judgment is

written in Revelation 20:11-15. The time is future, after the millennium and the judgment of the wicked angels. The place is in heaven. Who will be the judge? It is written that those who are judged will stand before God, so that many assume that God the Father is alluded to in this description. Even were the reading accurate, Christ is God, and to Him all judgment has been committed, as was stated earlier. The reading of verse 12 should be, "And I saw the dead, small and great, stand before the throne" rather than "stand before God." Christ is the judge. Those who are to be judged are the dead, small and great—all those who have died without faith in God and His gracious provision, in Christ, of salvation and life everlasting. Trusting in themselves, they will be judged out of the things written in the books of record, according to their works. And because their names are not written in the book of life and their works in which they trust cannot be good enough, they will all—every one of them—be cast into the lake of fire (v. 15).

The Judgment Seat of Christ

The first of these seven judgments, the judgment of sin, relates to the church in that, apart from Calvary and the empty tomb, there would be no church, no body and bride of Christ. But that judgment is past. The second of the seven judgments, the believer's self-judgment, relates to the church too; for it is believers that compose the true church. Believers come under this judgment. As they judge themselves, their fellowship with God now and usefulness in His service on earth are determined. This judgment is present.

It is the third of the seven judgments, which is future, that requires attention at this point. It will affect every believer in the Lord Jesus Christ; "for we must all appear before the judgment seat of Christ; that every one may receive the things done in his body, according to that he hath done, whether it be good or bad" (II CORINTHIANS 5:10).

In I Corinthians 3 it is revealed that the foundation stone of the Christian life is Jesus Christ and faith in Him (v. 11). Upon this foundation the believer builds, his works being likened to gold, silver, precious stones, wood, hay, and stubble (v. 12). In the day of this judgment every one's work will be made manifest—not as to its size or the acclaim that it receives, but "of what sort it is" (v. 13). The believer's works will be tested by fire. If these works come through the fire, he will receive a reward. If they are consumed by the fire, he will suffer loss. But observe that "he himself shall be saved, yet so as by fire" (vv. 14-15). The matter of sin is not judged at the judgment seat of Christ. Sin was judged at Calvary. This judgment is of those who are believers, who have been redeemed. It is a judgment of what has been done with the life after receiving the new life in Christ.

The expression, "judgment seat," is rendered from a Greek noun, *bēma*, which denotes a tribunal, that is, a place where a judge sits to administer justice—awards or penalties. At the completion of an event in the Olympic games, for example, the medals are given to the winners, who stand before the *bēma* where the appointed judge presents the awards. So believers will stand before the tribunal of Christ after the translation of the church to receive His awards in accord with how they have run the race.

The test is by fire, as it were. Gold, silver, and precious stones may be melted in the fire, but they will survive it. And all the dross—any element of man and the flesh that has entered into the works—will be burned away, so that these works will be wholly pure in the end. Wood, hay, and stubble will burn. Nothing but ashes will be left after the testing.

Gold may be said to represent divine majesty and holiness. Whatever the believer does in this life that reflects the perfections and grace of God, will react to the fire as does gold.

Silver is the metal of redemption, so that faithful witness concerning the saving grace of God in Christ is a work that will withstand the judging fire.

Precious stones may typify other Christian virtues—obedience, the prayer life, love and compassion towards our fellows, and the like.

Wood is utilitarian and decorative. It has many uses, but in the flames it burns to ashes. Some religious deeds that are not performed for the glory of God will be consumed before the tribunal.

Hay nourishes. Even some preaching of the Word may be like hay insofar as reward is concerned. This message, for example, expounds the Scriptures by which some hearers may be blessed.

But if my purpose in writing it is to make a name for myself, or to receive an honorarium to enlarge my bank account, this particular work will not withstand the fire and will not receive a reward.

Stubble is absolutely useless for anything. How frequently we allow ourselves to become occupied in so-called church work which is of no value whatever to the cause of Christ!

Gold, silver, precious stones. Wood, hay, stubble. When the church stands before the judgment seat of Christ, the former will abide, the latter will be burned.

I know that, once we are in the presence of the Lord, it is generally thought that all will be joy and that there will be no grief. I am not sure that this is wholly true. The Lord Jesus Himself knew grief on earth; He was grieved at the hardness of men's hearts. And the Holy Spirit is grieved when we resist Him. Joy will indeed be the predominant emotion of life with the Lord; but I suspect that, when our works are made manifest at the tribunal, some grief will be mixed with the joy, and we shall know shame as we suffer loss. But we shall rejoice also as we realize that the rewards given will be another example of the grace of our Lord; for at best we are unprofitable servants.

The Elders in Heaven

In chapters 2 and 3 of the Revelation the history of the church on earth is given. Immediately thereafter the Apostle John takes his readers into heaven; and there a scene is enacted that bears upon the rewards distributed at the *bēma*. For John sees in heaven a throne, and One seated upon the throne whose majesty is described in language of splendor. "And round about the throne were four and twenty thrones; and upon the thrones I saw four and twenty elders sitting, clothed in white raiment; and they had on their heads crowns of gold" (REVELATION 4:4). Who are these elders and what are the crowns on their heads?

There have been all sorts of suggestions concerning the identity of the elders. Some have proposed that they are the overcomers mentioned in chapters 2 and 3. Others submit that they represent the principalities and powers of Ephesians 1:21 and Colossians 1:16. Still others state that the elders are the angels and authori-

ties of I Peter 3:22. And a few think that they are incapable of
identification.

There is not a single place in all the Scriptures where angels are
referred to as elders, but there are many, many instances of men
being thus designated, from Genesis to I Peter. And twelve times
in the Revelation the word "elders" is used where, by the context,
they are always distinguished from celestial beings. Never, prior to
Revelation 4, are elders seen in heaven, but always on earth.

The Apostle John was not the only one of God's servants to
view heavenly scenes.

Isaiah, in the year that King Uzziah died, "saw also the Lord
sitting upon a throne, high and lifted up" (ISAIAH 6:1). The ancient seer perceived many wonders in this vision. And he observed
the seraphim, angelic beings who cried one to another, "Holy,
holy, holy is the Lord of hosts; the whole earth is full of his
glory." But Isaiah saw no four and twenty elders sitting upon four
and twenty thrones.

Ezekiel, the son of Buzi, when he was by the river Chebar in
the land of the Chaldeans, had visions of God in which he saw
"the likeness of a throne" and "the appearance and likeness of the
glory of the Lord" (EZEKIEL 1:26, 28). In that experience the
ancient prophet beheld many marvelous things. He saw four living
creatures, celestial beings whom John gazed upon centuries later.
But Ezekiel did not look upon four and twenty thrones occupied
by four and twenty elders.

Prior to the occasion when John was carried into heaven, as it
were, and saw the twenty-four elders seated before the throne, he
had a vision, on the Isle of Patmos, in which he gazed into the
glory to behold astonishing things (REVELATION 1:9-20). But he
then saw no such thrones and elders as he later beheld.

Why did Isaiah, who looked upon the seraphim, fail to see the
four and twenty elders? Why did Ezekiel, who observed the four
living creatures, miss seeing four and twenty elders seated upon
thrones? Why did not John, in his earlier vision, take note of their
presence? Because the elders were not there yet! Not until the
experience of Revelation 4, when the Apostle was taken in vision
up into heaven, did he perceive the four and twenty elders seated
around the throne of the Lord.

Who are these elders clothed in white raiment and adorned with crowns of gold? They represent, unless I am badly mistaken, the raptured church after her receipt of the awards given out at the *bēma* of Christ. These golden crowns are symbolic of the crowns of glory, righteousness, rejoicing, and life promised to believers for faithfulness of one sort or another (PHILIPPIANS 4:1; I THESSALONIANS 2:19; II TIMOTHY 4:8; JAMES 1:12; I PETER 5:4; REVELATION 2:10).

The church has here been caught up to meet Christ in the air. The church stands before the judgment seat of Christ and receives her rewards. Then the church, enthroned around the throne of the Lord, perhaps the *bēma* itself, beholds His glory and majesty there. And "the four and twenty elders fall down before Him that sat upon the throne, and worship Him that liveth forever and ever, and cast their crowns before the throne, saying, Thou art worthy, O Lord, to receive glory and honour and power; for thou hast created all things, and for Thy pleasure they are and were created" (REVELATION 4:10-11).

Conclusion

There is another judgment at which the true church will be present. The church will not be under judgment but will share in the administration of it. For Christ will pronounce judgment as King of kings and Lord of lords, and the church is to reign with Him.

At the judgment of the great white throne, when the wicked dead of all ages will be judged to eternal condemnation, I think that the church will stand behind the Judge as He metes out the judgment. I wonder if, when we gaze out upon the vast sea of faces of men and women who are utterly hopeless, we shall observe among them some to whom we failed to bear witness concerning the saving grace of the Lord Jesus Christ! For there will be no hope for them then. It will be too late.

Dear friend, be sure that you are among the redeemed and that your name is written in the Lamb's book of life. And may God make those of us who do believe in Christ faithful in our witness to Him.

III

The Church and the Tribulation

E. Schuyler English

A number of years ago there appeared in the *New Yorker* an account of a singular incident that illustrates aptly the apathetic attitude of a great many people who, if they read the Bible at all, do so with their eyes only and not with their minds and hearts.

The article of which I speak told of a Long Island resident who was able one day to satisfy a desire that he had had for several years—to order from Abercrombie & Fitch an extremely sensitive barometer. When the instrument arrived at his home he was disappointed to discover that the indicating needle appeared to be stuck pointing to the sector marked "Hurricane." After shaking the barometer vigorously several times—never a good idea with a sensitive mechanism—the new owner wrote a scathing letter to the store and, on the following morning, on the way to his office in New York, mailed it. That evening he returned to Long Island to find not only the barometer missing but his house as well! The needle of the instrument had been pointed correctly. There was a hurricane. The month was September, 1938.

We smile with incredulity that this man had so little faith in a valuable instrument that he purchased at considerable expense. Yet how many there are who seem to regard the clear fingers of prophetic Scriptures with indifference, even disdain! The Bible predicts the second advent of Christ, and points with clear statements to certain phenomena that will attend that event—wars and rumors of wars, nation rising against nation, Israel's rehabitation of her ancient land, federations of nations, earthquakes and pestilences, and unbelief, blasphemy, and apostasy in the professing church. Yet the world and great segments of the church pursue their regular course of life, eating and drinking, marrying and giving in marriage, as they did in the days of Noah, the business of living going on as usual.

It should be borne in mind that the second coming of Christ will occur in two phases: (1) our Lord will come to meet His church in the air—a living generation of believers and the dead in Christ who will be raised in an instant; and (2) the Lord will return to the earth itself in power and great glory. The phenomena to which we have alluded will take place prior to His return to the earth. The question is: Will they of necessity occur before He catches His church into the air to meet Him? Is Christ's coming for His church imminent, or must certain prophetic judgments take place before the church can expect to hear the Lord's call into His presence?

The Tribulation

To discover the answer to the problem it is necessary, first, to refer to one of the great prophecies of the Bible, generally known as the prophecy of Daniel's seventy weeks, which is written in Daniel 9:24-27. The prediction is recorded by Daniel, but the words were actually spoken by the Angel Gabriel, whom the Lord sent to Daniel in answer to the prophet's prayer of supplication.

Gabriel told Daniel that seventy weeks were determined upon his (Daniel's) people, Israel, before an end of sins could be made, and to make reconciliation, bring in everlasting righteousness, and anoint the Most Holy. The expression, "seventy weeks," denotes *seventy periods of seven*. History shows that these "weeks" are weeks of seven years each rather than seven days each, or an overall period of 490 years.

Sixty-nine of the weeks of years—that is, 483 years—passed between the decree of Artaxerxes for the rebuilding of Jerusalem following the Babylonian captivity, and the cutting off of Messiah the Prince, that is, the crucifixion of Christ (vv. 24-26). Since only sixty-nine weeks of prophetic years have been fulfilled, that leaves one week of years, seven years, still to come. For since the crucifixion of Christ and attendant events, man has entered and lived in a parenthetic period, the church age. At the end of this church age, the prediction concerning Daniel's final week will be fulfilled. It will begin when the prince of the people who destroyed Jerusalem and the sanctuary, in A.D. 70, makes a covenant with the Jewish people for a seven-year period (v. 27). In the middle of the week, that is, after three and a half years, this prince will break his covenant with the Jews, cause a cessation of sacrifice and oblation in the temple, and persecute the Jews unmercifully.

It is to this period that our Lord referred in His Olivet Discourse: "When ye therefore see the abomination of desolation spoken of by Daniel, the prophet, stand in the holy place (who readeth, let him understand), then let them which be in Judaea flee into the mountains . . . For then shall be great tribulation, such as was not since the beginning of the world to this time, no, nor ever shall be" (MATTHEW 24:15-16, 21). This period, which is equivalent to Daniel's seventieth week and composes a great part of the Book of the Revelation, is generally termed "The Tribulation."

I have given here no more than a cursory diagnosis of Gabriel's message to Daniel, but it is sufficient to establish that Daniel's seventieth week is yet future, that it is identical with the period of tribulation predicted by our Lord, and that its duration is seven years.

The Tribulation will be a time of unparalleled destruction of life and property, especially the latter half of it. It will be not only an era of trial for Israel but also of catastrophic judgment upon Gentiles, culminating in the world-wide devastation of the power and authority of the nations (REVELATION 18-19). During this seven-year period the calamities of Christ's Olivet Discourse will come to pass: nation rising against nation, and kingdom against kingdom; famines, pestilences, and earthquakes; betrayal, deception, and iniquity; blasphemy, false prophets, and false Christs (MATTHEW 24). Apostasy will increase, as will immorality and dishonesty (I TIMOTHY 4; II TIMOTHY 3). Trumpets will sound for judgment (REVELATION 8-11) and bowls of wrath will be poured out (REVELATION 16).

No wonder it is said of the Tribulation that since the beginning of the world to this time there has never been anything like it, nor ever will be. It will be "immediately after the tribulation of those days" that Christ will return to the earth in power and glory to destroy His enemies and to reign over the earth during the millennium (MATTHEW 24:29-30). Will it be at this same time, after the Tribulation, that the Lord Jesus will come and meet His raptured church in the air?

The Rapture

Before answering the question as to when the translation of the church will take place, it will be profitable to define what the rapture is.

There are a number of allusions in the New Testament to the translation of the church. Among the most familiar are John 14:2-3, where our Lord says: "I will come again and receive you unto myself"; I Corinthians 15:51-54, where Paul writes: "Behold, I show you a mystery: We shall not all sleep, but we shall all be changed in a moment, in the twinkling of an eye, at the last trump; for the trumpet shall sound, and the dead shall be raised incorruptible, and we shall all be changed"; and the opening words of a paragraph in the Apostle's second letter to the Thessalonian church, where he says: "Now I beseech you, brethren, by the coming of our Lord Jesus Christ, and by our gathering together unto him" (II THESSALONIANS 2:1). But by far the fullest revelation concerning the rapture of the Church is the well-known description in I Thessalonians 4:13-17.

In verses 13 and 14 Paul gives his readers an expression of reassurance. He does not want them to be ignorant about those of their number who have died since they became believers in Christ. The living need not sorrow as others do who have no hope in Christ. For all who believe the gospel, that is, that Christ died for our sins and rose again, may have the assurance that the Lord will bring with Him their loved ones who have died in faith. There will be reunion.

In verses 15 to 17 he tells how this will come to pass. First, observe that what the Apostle tells the Thessalonians is not a figment of his imagination. What he writes he writes "by the word of the Lord" (v. 15). This is no hallucination; it is revelation.

Second, notice that when the Lord comes for His own, those who are to be caught up into His presence without dying are not going to go ahead of those who have died in Christ. "We which are alive and remain unto the coming of the Lord shall not prevent [precede] them which are asleep" (v. 15).

Third, it is not an apparition that will be seen at that time. Neither is the coming of the Lord another way of saying that the Holy Spirit or an angel will come to believers in some special manifestation. Paul writes: "For the Lord himself shall descend from heaven with a shout, with the voice of the archangel, and with the trump of God" (v. 16).

Fourth, believers who have died will be raised from the dead—raised before the translation of the living believers. "The dead in Christ shall rise first" (v. 16).

Fifth, all together—those who have been raised and those who are alive—will be caught up to meet the Lord in the air (v. 17).

And sixth, "so shall we ever be with the Lord" (v. 17). In His presence we shall be like Him, we shall serve Him, and we shall reign with Him.

An astonishing and dramatic event will take place one day. For in a moment, just as long as it takes an eyelid to fall and rise, graves will be opened and resurrected saints, together with myriads of living believers, will be caught up into the air to meet the Lord. Consternation and confusion will develop among the millions left here on earth. Then some will begin to recognize that what has occurred is what they have heard about in a church service or through the testimony of a loved one, but they neither heeded it nor believed it.

The Time of the Rapture in Relation to the Tribulation

No man knows the day or the hour of the Lord's coming—either for His church or in glory to reign on earth. There is, however, intimation in the Scriptures as to the time of the church's translation in relation to the Tribulation. And there are four schools of thought regarding this matter, called posttribulationism, midtribulationism, pretribulationism, and partial rapturism.

Posttribulationists believe that the rapture of the church will not take place until after the Tribulation. They hold that the second advent of Christ will be one sweeping event: the church will be caught up into the air to meet the Lord and will return to the earth with Him immediately.

Midtribulationists believe that the church will be caught up halfway through the Tribulation, at the time that the coming prince of Daniel 9:27, the beast out of the sea of Revelation 13:1, the man of sin of II Thessalonians 2:3, breaks his convenant with the Jewish people.

Pretribulationists—and most of us here are of this school—hold that the Lord will call His church to Himself prior to the Tribulation, before the first seal of Revelation 6 is broken.

Partial rapturists believe that only a portion of the church will be taken at the rapture at the beginning of the Tribulation—only those who are watching and waiting for the Lord, only those who are looking for Him.

It is somewhat unfair to dismiss any of these views, all of which are held by godly men and women, in a sentence or two. But the limitations of time in an essay of this kind compel brevity.

In regard to the partial rapture teaching, the most telling answer to the doctrine, in my judgment, is written in I Corinthians 15:51-52, unquestionably one of the key passages on the rapture, where twice the expression, "we shall all be changed," is used. "We shall not all sleep, but we shall all be changed, in a moment, in the twinkling of an eye . . . for the trumpet shall sound, and the dead shall be raised incorruptible, and we shall all be changed." We shall *all* be changed. There is no partial rapturism in this passage. Like salvation, translation is also by grace. All who believe will be saved. All who are saved will either be raised or translated into heaven without dying.

The posttribulationists are of two schools. Some teach that the tribulation is already here, as it has been for some time—thus the church is now going through the Tribulation. Others hold that the Tribulation is future, but in the light of our Lord's declaration, "In the world ye shall have tribulation" (JOHN 16:33), and of the statement in Revelation 20:4-6 that the martyred saints of the tribulation period are raised as part of the first resurrection to live and reign with Christ, the church must go through the Tribulation. The posttibulationists also cite Matthew 24:29-31 where, immediately after the tribulation, the coming Son of man sends His angels with the sound of a trumpet to gather His elect from the four winds; and Matthew 25:31-46, where Christ, coming in His glory, gathers all nations for the judgment of the sheep and the goats. It is proposed by the posttribulationists that to hold the pretribulationist view is simply wishful thinking, a desire to escape suffering. There are other Scriptures that these brethren point to, but rather than endeavor to refute them now I shall seek to show later why I believe no part of the church will pass through any part of the Tribulation.

Midtribulationists, as has been mentioned, hold that the church will be caught up when the coming prince of the Gentiles breaks his covenant with the nation Israel. They point to Matthew 24 and affirm that in verses 4 to 14 prediction is made concerning the beginning of sorrows, whereas verses 15 to 28 make known the "great tribulation," and that it is in this period, the latter half of Daniel's seventieth week, that the church will escape.

The pretribulationists do not deny, and neither do the other schools, that there are problems. Nowhere in the references to the rapture is its time, in relation to the Tribulation, explicitly stated. There are intimations concerning this, however. I shall discuss three of them—one demonstrating that the translation of the church cannot be concomitant with Christ's return to the earth, and two establishing that the rapture must be before the Tribulaion.

First, it is obvious that the Lord returns to earth in power and glory "immediately after the tribulation of those days" (MATTHEW 24:29-31); that is, the period of the "great tribulation" that our Lord referred to earlier in His Olivet Discourse. It is then, too, when all nations are gathered before Him, that He will set the sheep on His right hand and the goats on His left (MATTHEW 25:31-46). The sheep will inherit the earthly kingdom (v. 34); the goats will be committed to "everlasting fire, prepared for the devil and his angels" (v. 41). This is, as has been said, immediately after the tribulation. If the rapture takes place at this time and all the blessed are caught up to be with Christ, whereas all the condemned are cast into everlasting fire, who are the sheep? Who will be left on earth to enter the millennial kingdom? A rapture at this time would leave the kingdom without an inhabitant, the King without a single subject. The rapture of the church cannot be coincident with Christ's return to the earth, that is, after the Tribulation.

Second, the coming Gentile prince of Daniel 9, the man of sin of II Thessalonians 2, will be revealed at the beginning of the Tribulation when the first seal of Revelation 6 is broken and the first of the four horsemen rides forth. There is One who restrains the appearance of the wicked one. Until the restrainer is taken out of the way, this son of perdition cannot enter the scene. Who is the One who restrains? Despite arguments to the contrary, it seems evident that the restrainer is the Holy Spirit, the One who acted in such a capacity even before the flood until God said, "My Spirit shall not always strive with man" (GENESIS 6:3).

The Holy Spirit came to dwell within the hearts of believers on the Day of Pentecost. And "if any man have not the Spirit of Christ he is none of his" (ROMANS 8:9). The Spirit is the earnest of the church's inheritance (EPHESIANS 1:14) by whom the church has been "sealed unto the day of redemption" (EPHESIANS 4:30). The Holy Spirit cannot be taken out of the way as a restraining influence while the church is on earth. When He is taken out of the way, the wicked one will be revealed (II THESSALONIANS 2:7-8). Therefore, since the man of sin makes his appearance at the beginning of Daniel's seventieth week, which is equivalent to the Tribulation, and the Holy Spirit is taken out of the way before the man of sin appears, the church also must be removed from this earthly scene before the Tribulation begins.

And third, where there is rapture there is resurrection. The two definitive Scriptures concerning the translation of the church are, as has been stated, I Corinthians 15:51-54 and I Thessalonians 4:13-17. In both of them there are resurrection of the dead in Christ and translation of a living generation of believers. The passages that relate to Christ's return to the earth after the Tribulation speak of a gathering on earth of God's people, but not of resurrection or translation. In the prophecy of Revelation 20, concerning the martyred saints who are to be raised after the Tribulation, there is no translation. Midway through the Tribulation there is no suggestion of resurrection and rapture; in fact, the church is not alluded to in the Revelation after the breaking of the first seal, which introduces the Tribulation.

Conclusion

At least ten times in the Revelation the Tribulation is spoken of as a period of wrath—"the wrath of the Lamb" and "the wrath of God." But "God hath not appointed us [the true church] to wrath, but to obtain salvation by our Lord Jesus Christ, who died for us that, whether we wake or sleep, we should live together with Him. Wherefore comfort yourselves together, and edify one another, even as also ye do" (I THESSALONIANS 5:9-11). No part of the true church will be obliged to undergo any part of the wrath of God. "Wherefore comfort one another with these words."

IV

Israel's Conflict and the World's Zero Hour

Charles Lee Feinberg

"Zero hour" is the modern expression for the hour of attack, the hour of decision, the hour of conflict, the hour of crisis, the hour in which an ordeal is to begin. The world is unquestionably rushing on to just such an hour. Important events of the past few years may have looked like this zero hour, but the Bible clearly defines that time, so that no one need be in doubt. It is the hour in which the death rattle will be heard in the throat of the nations who have turned from God and His will.

The disclosure of this important period in world history is found in Zechariah 12:1-13:1. This great prophetic portion sets forth, first of all,

THE COLOSSAL CONFEDERACY.

The burden of the word of the Lord concerning Israel. Thus saith the Lord, who stretcheth forth the heavens, and layeth the foundation of the earth, and formeth the spirit of man within him: Behold, I will make Jerusalem a cup of reeling unto all the peoples round about, and upon Judah also shall it be in the siege against Jerusalem. And it shall come to pass in that day, that I will make Jerusalem a burdensome stone for all the peoples; all that burden themselves with it shall be sore wounded; and all the nations of the earth shall be gathered together against it. . . . And it shall come to pass in that day, that I will seek to destroy all the nations that come against Jerusalem (ZECHARIAH 12:1-3, 9, ASV).

It is made clear at the outset that the prophecy concerns Israel, that is, Judah and Jerusalem primarily. The One who is foretelling

these tremendous events is none other than the Omnipotent One
in the realm of heaven, on earth, and among men. Jerusalem, from
which has come so much of the prophetic utterance of the Word
of God, and from which center salvation for all the world has
flowed out through the many centuries, will become a basin of
reeling to all the peoples and nations that dare to besiege her.
Many have been the attacks on the city of Jerusalem. It has
suffered destruction more times than any other important city in
the world. The nations, bent on defying God and His program,
will seek a last chance to annihilate that city from which the
Messiah Himself will reign in His Davidic kingdom. If other attempts to obliterate Jerusalem have been a sad failure, this last
onslaught will be the most futile of all. Instead of inflicting permanent harm on Jerusalem, the invading forces will be sent reeling. They will be made to stagger as a drunkard. The Scriptures on
more than one occasion show that a visitation from God upon
ungodliness is like being intoxicated with a poisonous liquid
(ISAIAH 51:17-20; JEREMIAH 25:15-16). Today we speak of one
who has been battered and bruised in a conflict as being "punch-
drunk." Such will be the condition of the nations confederated
against the capital city of Jerusalem. The text of Zechariah states
that the invaders will be "all the peoples" and "all the nations of
the earth." These armies will be in well-defined alliances, as predicted in the Old Testament prophetic oracles. There will be the
group of nations in the south of Europe in the revived Roman
Empire, spoken of in Daniel 2 and 7, and Revelation 13 and 17;
the Assyrian power of Daniel 11; the powers of the north of
Europe, Russia, and Germany of Ezekiel 38 and 39; and the kings
of the East or the Orient of Revelation 16. All the nations will be
infected with the virus of anti-Semitism in that day.

There is an ascending climax in thought in the words of the
prophet. Jerusalem is likened to a basin of reeling, which renders
powerless; she is then compared to a burdensome stone which
actually wounds and bruises. But there is more in store for the
ungodly; in addition to the wounding, there will be destruction.
This will be the world's decisive hour. The nations, sadly enough,
will find God's final answer to their threat over Israel, His people.

A preacher once said: "When you stand and look at the sweeping flames of a prairie fire on an autumnal day, stretching leagues

away, or at night, throwing a lurid light into the broad heaven above, you do not suppose that those vast flames were put there. The negligent hunter, after his evening meal, sat smoking his pipe; he knocked a spark out of it, and it kindled, and grew, and he watched it, thinking that he might at any moment subdue it by the stroke of his boot; but it escaped him, and ran, and spread here and there and everywhere, and swung on, and the wind caught it and nourished it, and it laughed and roared and crackled as it sped along, growing wider and more fierce, consuming harvest, fence, hut, and hovel. It took care of itself after it was once kindled. It had in itself multiplying power." Thus it will be with the revealed rebellion of the nations against God and their confederacy against Israel.

In the second place, our passage deals with

THE CONQUERING CAPTIVES.

In that day, saith the Lord, I will smite every horse with terror, and his rider with madness; and I will open mine eyes upon the house of Judah, and will smite every horse of the peoples with blindness. And the chieftains of Judah shall say in their heart, The inhabitants of Jerusalem are my strength in the Lord of hosts their God. In that day will I make the chieftains of Judah like a pan of fire among wood, and like a flaming torch among sheaves; and they shall devour all the peoples round about, on the right hand and on the left; and they of Jerusalem shall yet again dwell in their own place, even in Jerusalem. The Lord also shall save the tents of Judah first, that the glory of the house of David and the glory of the inhabitants of Jerusalem be not magnified above Judah. In that day shall the Lord defend the inhabitants of Jerusalem; and he that is feeble among them at that day shall be as David; and the house of David shall be as God, as the angel of the Lord before them (ZECHARIAH 12:4-8, ASV).

Zechariah foretells that God will give the victory to His people in a twofold way: (1) He will personally overpower the enemy; and (2) He will empower Israel to triumph over their enemies. The plagues of terror, madness, and blindness, mentioned in

Deuteronomy 28:28 for disobedience, will fall upon the enemy suddenly and simultaneously. Horses are mentioned prominently, because cavalry has always held a large place in eastern warfare. God will paralyze the forces of the enemy. While He blinds the eyes of the enemy, He will open His own in compassion and protection on Israel.

Then the Lord will so work in the hearts of the leaders of Israel that they will realize and admit that the victory was not because of their own strength. They will give credit to the Lord alone. A million tons of water pass over Niagara Falls every hour. Could man stop that mighty torrent? Impossible. Yet God did it. One winter He froze those raging waters into solid ice. His power is boundless. Power belongeth unto the Lord, as the Psalmist declares, and He will impart it to His beleaguered people. In vivid colors the prophet paints the picture of the victory granted His people over the foe; it will be as an irresistible fire leaping its unhindered way among wood or sheaves of grain. Their success will issue in the deliverance and settlement of the people in their God-appointed place. In the actual victory the defenseless country will be delivered before the well-defended capital, so that the city of Jerusalem with its inhabitants will not boast over the outlying districts, but both must acknowledge the victory as from God. Even the weakest in the nation will be strengthened of the Lord to do exploits like the greatest national hero, David, and the mighty ones will be as irresistible as a force from the Lord Himself.

Cecil Rhodes, the great empire builder of South Africa, said: "Most men are after peacock's feathers, but I'm after power." How different from the Lord God Almighty with whom is all power.

Finally, this important series of events issues in

THE CLEANSING CONFESSION.

And I will pour upon the house of David, and upon the inhabitants of Jerusalem, the spirit of grace and of supplication; and they shall look unto me whom they have pierced; and they shall mourn for him, as one mourneth for his only son, and shall be in bitterness for him, as one that is in bitterness for his first-born. In that day shall there be a great mourning in Jerusalem, as the mourning of Hadad-rimmon in the valley of Megiddon. And the land shall mourn, every family apart; the family of the house of David apart, and their wives apart; the family of the house of Nathan apart, and their wives apart; the family of the house of Levi apart, and their wives apart; the family of the Shimeites apart, and their wives apart; all the families that remain, every family apart, and their wives apart. In that day there shall be a fountain opened to the house of David and to the inhabitants of Jerusalem, for sin and for uncleanness (ZECHARIAH 12:10–13:1, ASV).

Once the world confederacy has been dealt with, the Lord resumes His national dealings with Israel. Where their Lord and Messiah was rejected, there God begins His work of restoration. It will be at Jerusalem. The divine order is plain: first, conviction of sin for their rejecting and piercing their King, and then the presentation of their Messiah to them before their eyes. Like unbelieving Thomas, they will not believe until they see His hands. Then their mourning will know no bounds; it will be like the most intense personal sorrow as that for the death of the only son or first-born. It will be comparable to the greatest public calamity, as in the death of the godly King Josiah in the battle with Pharaohnecho of Egypt (II CHRONICLES 35:22). The death of this godly monarch marked the sunset of the Judean kingdom. The sorrow will be national and individual too: each will want to be alone in the presence of God. All the families in the land, from the highest to the lowest, will be included in this deep mourning and conviction over sin. Then will be brought about the glorious result: a purified and cleansed Israel that will avail itself of the fountain opened for them at Calvary for sin and for uncleanness.

Years ago in Boston, there was a German who had received a wound in the Great War. Whenever he heard lively music he could not refrain from joining, being a musician of ability, and whenever his emotions were stirred, the wound would open; it could not be permanently stanched. Powers of earth and hell have conspired to obliterate the five bleeding wounds, but still there is "a fountain open for sin" from Messiah's work on Calvary. Thank God, anyone can avail himself of this provision now.

V

God's Plan for Lasting Peace

Charles Lee Feinberg

The portion for our present consideration is Zechariah 9:1-10 (ASV), which reads as follows:

> The burden of the word of the Lord upon the land of Hadrach, and Damascus shall be its resting-place (for the eye of man and of all the tribes of Israel is toward the Lord); and Hamath, also, which bordereth thereon; Tyre and Sidon, because they are very wise. And Tyre did build herself a stronghold, and heaped up silver as the dust, and fine gold as the mire of the streets. Behold, the Lord will dispossess her, and he will smite her power in the sea; and she shall be devoured with fire. Ashkelon shall see it, and fear; Gaza also, and shall be sore pained; and Ekron, for her expectation shall be put to shame; and the king shall perish from Gaza, and Ashkelon shall not be inhabited. And a bastard shall dwell in Ashdod, and I will cut off the pride of the Philistines. And I will take away his blood out of his mouth, and his abominations from between his teeth; and he also shall be a remnant for our God; and he shall be as a chieftain in Judah, and Ekron as a Jebusite. And I will encamp about my house against the army, that none pass through or return; and no oppressor shall pass through them any more: for now have I seen with mine eyes. Rejoice greatly, O daughter of Zion; shout, O daughter of Jerusalem: behold, thy king cometh unto thee; he is just, and having salvation; lowly, and riding upon an ass, even upon a colt the foal of an ass. And I will cut off the chariot from Ephraim, and the horse from Jerusalem; and the battle bow shall be cut off; and he shall speak peace unto the nations: and his dominion shall be from sea to sea, and from the River to the ends of the earth.

The first eight verses of this passage set forth the conquests of Alexander the Great. Coming from Greece, he marched down the Phoenician and Palestinian coast, capturing in turn Damascus, Sidon, Tyre, and Gaza. Neither the Phoenicians, nor the Syrians, nor the Philistines escaped the rod of his wrath. But he passed by Jerusalem more than once without harming it, a manifest token of God's protection of His land, His temple, and His people. The prophet Zechariah now, by the prophetic law of suggestion, is directed of the Spirit of God to see a still greater deliverance for his people and the nations of the world. The prophets of God were so filled with expectations of the Messiah that they turned from every deliverance, no matter how small or insignificant, to the last and greatest of all. From an earthly conqueror of great ruthlessness and military prowess, Alexander the Great, Zechariah gazes upon the coming King of the whole earth. The remaining verses of the chapter (vv. 11-17) are occupied with the Maccabean Wars of the second century B.C. Inserted between two martial scenes, verses 9 and 10 furnish us a short sketch, a thumbnail sketch, of God's plan for lasting and permanent peace.

Zechariah clearly gives us all the elements of the program. He points out, first of all,

THE AGENT OF PEACE.

The prophet calls upon all in the nation to rejoice and shout. The coming of this One is not attended with fear for His people, as was so often the case with foreign invaders. His advent is the cause for great rejoicing. It should be remembered that God never asks man to rejoice in this world's fleeting pleasures. Israel, as she sees the approach of the King of Peace, is enjoined to great exultation. The One coming is designated as Israel's King, her very own, the long-awaited, long-promised, long-prophesied One. He comes to Israel, that is, He is of Israel as to the flesh, but He appears to them from the Father (ROMANS 1:3, 4). And not only *to* them, but, as the original wording will allow, *for* them, for their eternal good. His coming is not for His own profit or self-aggrandizement, as with earthly rulers.

If one were to inquire of a normal congregation the three characteristics of a suitable world ruler, they would present qualifications far different from the ones the Spirit of God foretells here. First and foremost, He will be just or righteous. The prime and indispensable prerequisite in a true ruler and the foundation principle for true and lasting peace is righteousness. He is altogether righteous. There is an unbreakable link between righteousness and peace. Isaiah (32:17, ASV) stated: "And the work of righteousness shall be peace; and the effect of righteousness, quietness and confidence for ever." (Compare also PSALM 45:6, 7; ISAIAH 11:3-5; and JEREMIAH 23:5.) He is animated in every act by righteousness. How odious to God is an unjust and unrighteous ruler. Peace must be grounded and founded in justice. This King Messiah, the Lord Jesus Christ, will act accordingly.

Furthermore, the coming King, the Agent of peace, will be vitally related to the question of salvation. The world's peace depends upon a Saviour and His salvation. He is endowed with, entrusted with salvation, with help from God. Only a thoroughly righteous person could be the channel for mediating the righteousness of God to a sinful and rebellious world. Finally, He is to be lowly. Here He stands in grand contradistinction to the haughty and proud rulers of the earth. The thought of lowliness and meekness with peaceful intent is brought out further by the manner of His travel. He comes without pomp or earthly splendor. It is a matter of record that after the time of Solomon there is not one example of a king or distinguished personage riding upon an ass. The One who had not where to lay His head, in order that we might rest our heads upon the bosom of the Father whence He proceeded, did not conceal His poverty nor His lowliness. Pride was as foreign to Him as it is common to the world's kings.

It is told that a painter called upon a fellow-artist and, finding him out, asked for a pencil and paper, and left a picture. When the friend returned, he said immediately, "Rubens has been here. None but he could have drawn such a picture." We say of Zechariah's portrait that only the Spirit of God could have drawn it, and only Christ can be meant by it. But, we are told, He did not bring about lasting world peace when He came to earth. True, but in that first and lowly coming He laid the basis by His death for that peace of which we read in the next verse.

Secondly, the prophet, in outlining God's plan for lasting peace, presents

THE METHOD OF PEACE.

The picture of the Messiah in verse 10, alongside that in verse 9, was so puzzling to Jewish commentators that they resorted to an evasive theory of the two Messiahs, Messiah the Son of Joseph who comes in lowliness, and Messiah the Son of David who comes in power and glory. Zechariah 12:10 proves conclusively that there is but one Messiah. The One who was pierced and suffered on earth is the One who comes in power and majesty as King. Between verses 9 and 10 of our chapter have come all the centuries of the Christian era. A similar prophetic parenthesis is found in Isaiah 61:1, 2 and Daniel 9:24-27, among other references.

Having laid the foundation for all peace in the blood of His Cross, He now puts into effect peace for all the world. First, He destroys all instruments of warfare from His people, Ephraim and Jerusalem, and by so much from all the nations. See a similar connection in Isaiah 9:4-6 and 2:1-4. No defenses for carnal reliance will be left. All symbols of earthly might will be brought to nothing. This will be done not by the meek Lamb, but by the Lamb in wrath, the Lion roaring out of Zion. (Compare JOEL 3:16.)

But there is a constructive phase to His method of peace, as well as a destructive aspect. The Messiah will speak peace to the nations. What a pronouncement! What a message! What good news for an ineffective United Nations with its Security (?) Council! The prophet does not mean that He will speak peaceably or teach peace, but by an authoritative word He will command it. Just as He calmed the boisterous waves of the Sea of Galilee with a word, so He will still the strife in the hearts and lives of the nations in that day. Then will be accomplished by His word alone what men of earth have sought to do for centuries by the use of arms and warfare. True, He speaks peace to individuals now (EPHESIANS 2:17), but in that day He will speak peace to the nations. Therefore, He is the desire of all nations, though they know it not. (See HAGGAI 2:7.) Notice well that peace is not the result of peace conferences or of the preaching of social gospellers, but of the direct, immediate activity of the glorified Son of

God, the Prince of Peace. And it will be peace like a river, peace indeed, such as the world has never experienced before, though it has been sought after by scores of methods. Pursued diligently, it has yet never been attained.

Finally, the prophet reveals the last facet of the plan of God for lasting peace, when he indicates

THE KINGDOM OF PEACE.

Alexander the Great proudly believed that he had conquered all the world. One glance at a map of his day will show how far astray he really was. God has reserved universal dominion for One and for Him alone. His dominion is to be from sea to sea. Some commentators of the passage try to restrict these designations to Palestine itself, but the words "the ends of the earth" are not capable of such restriction or limitation. Definite articles are absent in the original. Furthermore, Psalm 72:8-11 shows in what sense these words are used. The passage reads:

> He shall have dominion also from sea to sea, And from the River unto the ends of the earth. They that dwell in the wilderness shall bow before him; And his enemies shall lick the dust. The kings of Tarshish and of the isles shall render tribute: The kings of Sheba and Seba shall offer gifts. Yea, all kings shall fall down before him; All nations shall serve him (ASV).

No matter how alluring or plausible the plan of an isolated peace may sound, it will never work. There can never be peace of a lasting nature on any continent as long as it is absent on another. The nations of earth and their rulers are absolutely powerless to give peace to their own land, let alone all the countries of the globe. God will give it to all lands alike. It is not peace at any price, but peace at infinite price, nothing less than the life of the Son of God. It is peace not for one, but for all.

Missionaries to India often tell of their visits to the Taj Mahal, that temple of unusual architectural beauty made of white marble. One of the peculiar features of the building is the number of arches it contains. A missionary, on nearing the entrance, was told by his guide that if he whispered even a word inside the building, it would reecho from every arch. Proceeding into the building, the missionary breathed the word "Jesus," and instantly the echoes resounded from every part of the building. The effect was electrifying and soul-inspiring. And when our Lord Jesus speaks the word "Peace" in that coming day, it will resound throughout the vault of heaven and the corridors of earth, and the earth with its teeming billions will thrill at the sound of it. Then, and not before then, will the earth know peace.

May that hour be hastened! May our zeal impel us to serve our Lord Jesus Christ acceptably among Jews and Gentiles! May our eyes be fixed upon Christ and Him alone and not upon the plans, futile plans, of men.

The End Time and the Resurrection of a Nation

Charles Lee Feinberg

The Old Testament prophet Ezekiel wrote during the time of Israel's exile in Babylon. Because his book is so full of visions and
predictions of judgment, many have felt free to neglect its message. But a close study of the contents of the prophecy will reveal
that the prophet of God did not confine himself to foretelling
judgment. There are in the pages of this book some of the most
glowing prophecies of future glory, blessing, and salvation. In the
thirty-sixth chapter Ezekiel turns to words of comfort, promise,
and blessing. Chapter 37 gives in vision form what was foretold in
direct prophetic address in the previous chapter. This is one of the
great chapters of the Bible, and one that is filled with hope and
bright prospect for Israel. The vision at the outset of the chapter
reads in this way:

> The hand of the Lord was upon me, and he brought me out
> in the Spirit of the Lord, and set me down in the midst of the
> valley; and it was full of bones. And he caused me to pass by
> them round about: and, behold, there were very many in the
> open valley; and, lo, they were very dry. And he said unto
> me, Son of man, can these bones live? And I answered, O
> Lord God, thou knowest. Again he said unto me, Prophesy
> over these bones, and say unto them, O ye dry bones, hear
> the word of the Lord. Thus saith the Lord God unto these
> bones: Behold, I will cause breath to enter into you, and ye
> shall live. And I will lay sinews upon you, and will bring up
> flesh upon you, and cover you with skin, and put breath in
> you, and ye shall live; and ye shall know that I am the Lord.
> So I prophesied as I was commanded: and as I prophesied,
> there was a noise, and, behold, an earthquake; and the bones

came together, bone to its bone. And I beheld, and, lo, there
were sinews upon them, and flesh came up, and skin covered
them above; but there was no breath in them. Then said, he
unto me, Prophesy unto the wind, prophesy, son of man, and
say to the wind, Thus saith the Lord God: Come from the
four winds, O breath, and breathe upon these slain, that they
may live. So I prophesied as he commanded me, and the
breath came into them, and they lived, and stood up upon
their feet, an exceeding great army (ASV).

The chapter before us has several important divisions. In the
first we have the disclosure of

THE VALLEY OF DRY BONES, verses 1-6.

The Lord Himself gives the prophet Ezekiel the vision we have
set before us in this chapter. The man of God is shown a valley
full of dry bones. The bones were many in number and very dry.
It is a picture of Israel brought to the place of lowest abasement,
of utter undoing. They had been bleaching in the valley for a long
period of time. When the Lord asked the prophet whether it were
possible for the bones to live again, the reply of the servant of
God indicated that it was humanly impossible. Only God could
bring about a deliverance from their condition. The purpose of the
vision is set forth: by the powerful Word of God a transformation
is to be brought about whereby the dry bones will live and all men,
especially Israel, will know the Person, power, and purpose of the
living God.
    The second portion of the chapter portrays

THE RESURRECTION OF THE DRY BONES, verses 7-10.

Through the preaching of the Word of the Lord, mighty and
supernatural movings transpire which bring about the plan of
God. The power of God's Word was such that the earth was made
to quake, and there was a mighty stirring among the dry bones.
Then sinews and flesh came upon the bones—all this accomplished through the irresistible Word of the living God. But there
was yet no breath in them. The return of Israel as a nation to the

land of their fathers is predicted in an unconverted condition. The Holy Spirit is not yet dwelling in power in their midst, and flowing through them in life-giving streams of blessing to the nations of the earth. But when the prophet prophesied to the wind, it entered the slain bodies and they came alive. The wind is the symbol of the Holy Spirit. Both Old and New Testaments bear witness to this fact (JOHN 3:8; EZEKIEL 36:27). Instead of lifeless, dry bones, the prophet now sees before him an exceedingly great army. It is a worldwide cemetery come alive! A nation is brought forth in a day! What a change this is from the picture at the beginning of the prophecy.

At this point in the record we are given

THE MEANING OF THE VISION, verses 11-14.

The key to the chapter is now presented. The bones are said to be the whole house of Israel. In exile and dispersion their cry has been that their hope has been cut off and lost. But at the beginning of the reign of Messiah, the Son of David, on His throne in Jerusalem, all Israel will be brought forth from their national graves, the Gentile peoples where they have been scattered. Once restored and regathered to the land, the Lord will bring them to Himself in repentance and faith. They will own their disobedience to the Lord and their rejection of His Messiah. The Holy Spirit will then be poured out upon them, and the result will be glorious indeed— a converted people regathered to their land and to their gracious God. How this vision throughout underscores the mighty power of God!

Many centuries ago a number of workmen might have been seen dragging a great marble block into the city of Florence in Italy. It had come from the famous marble quarries of Carrara, and was intended to be made into a statue of a great prophet. But it contained some flaws, and when Donatello, the celebrated Italian sculptor, saw it, he refused to accept it. So there it lay in the cathedral yard, a useless block. One day the great artist Michelangelo caught sight of the block. There rose up before his mind a thing of beauty, and he made a great resolution: he would make a great statue of it. It was a noble resolve and worthy of him. So he began the work. On the 11th day of September, 1500, early in the morning, Michelangelo began his work. There, day after day, week after week, he chiseled patiently away. He allowed no other hand to touch it. Months passed and still the work was unfinished. Not that he was idle, for he worked so hard at times that he slept with his working clothes on. And one day he said to a friend who thought that he was spending days and weeks of his time upon what seemed to be only trifles, "It is these trifles that make perfection."

Two more years passed away, and at last the statue was finished. On the 25th day of January, 1504, some of the first artists of the day assembled to see what Michelangelo had made of the despised and rejected block. They were a famous company. There was the architect Monciatto, and the great master Cosimo Roselli, and the renowned artist Botticelli, and San Gallo, the famous architect and engineer, and Leonardo da Vinci, then the first painter in Italy (of "Last Supper" fame), and there were also Filippino Lippi, and Pietro Perugino, the teacher of Raphael. The marvelous work was unveiled, and it stood for the first time challenging the admiration of one of the most famous gatherings of artists and architects that the world has ever seen. They all united in its praise, and their judgment was unanimous. It was a masterpiece. And as a masterpiece it deserved no common place; it must not be hidden. It must stand in the public square. It must be a tribute to the glory and fame of their renowned city. So it was decided. The statue weighed eighteen thousand pounds, and great care and skill were required to move it. For three days and nights it was watched by chosen guards as if it were a holy thing. On the 18th day of May, at dawn, it arrived in the great square of the city of Florence. There it stood for centuries; now it is placed within walls. Today it is in the Academy of Fine Arts of the city. It is the world-famous "David" of Michelangelo. It represents the Shepherd King, the sweet singer of Israel, in the strength of his youth. It is a sculptured poem of strength and is a masterpiece of art. But it is more than that. It is a lesson of the power of God. God can make of Simon, the swearing backslider, a Peter, the Apostle of Pentecost. He can make of cowardly Mark the standby of the great Apostle Paul. Yes, and He can make of a valley of dry bones, a mighty host of the Lord in a resurrected people of Israel.

The fourth division of the chapter points to

THE UNITED AND CONVERTED NATION, verses 15-23.

The sticks which the prophet is commanded to take to represent Judah, the southern kingdom, and Ephraim, the northern kingdom, remind us of the tribal rods in the days of Moses (NUMBERS 17:2). The bringing together of the two sticks represents in the simplest and clearest fashion the reuniting of the long-divided nation. The breach of Jeroboam's day is now finally healed. There will be one King in that day of Israel's glory and He will rule over but one kingdom. Israel will know their God in truth and He will be manifested as their Lord and God.

The last portion of the chapter makes mention of

THE DAVIDIC KING
AND THE SANCTIFIED PEOPLE, verses 24-28

The King that will rule over converted Israel is so worthy that our gaze is directed to Him once more. He is none other than David's greater Son, the Lord Jesus the Messiah (LUKE 1:36, 37). His people will dwell safely in their land permanently and securely with the Lord making His sanctuary in their midst. Then the nations will also come to know the Lord. After Israel is blessed, the whole world will receive blessing also (ACTS 15:16, 17).

What God will yet do for Israel nationally, He will do for any Jew now in the spiritual realm. He will bring him from spiritual rebellion and death to life in Himself through faith in the crucified Messiah. But He must have the penitent heart. A poor Jew once went to the temple with no lamb, no doves, no meal to sacrifice. He stood outside ashamed till he heard them sing Psalm 51: "A broken and a contrite heart, O God, Thou wilt not despise." He had that, so he went in. "Bless you, my son," said the venerable rabbi, "few come with such an offering!" God meets the penitent and contrite one with salvation always. He will do it now for you if you allow Him.

VII

The New Scofield Bible and
Missions to the Jews

Daniel Fuchs

The *New Scofield Reference Edition of the Holy Bible* is of distinctive benefit to the cause of Jewish missions. This is not surprising, because every member of the editorial committee is an outstanding Christian scholar who loves the Lord and His people, because he

> believes in and teaches the plenary inspiration and inerrancy of the Scriptures, the triune Godhead composed of the Father, the Son, and the Holy Spirit; the virgin birth and Deity of Christ; the necessity and efficacy of His atoning work; Christ's bodily resurrection and ascension; His imminent coming for His Church and His visible, premillennial return to the earth; the everlasting felicity of the redeemed; and the everlasting punishment of the lost (introduction to the 1967 edition, page v).

In other words, the theological stance of the new edition is foundational in the cause of Jewish missions. The study of this Bible will cause the student of the Scriptures to become intensely involved in the evangelization of the Jews.

Jewish missions are based on the premise that "the Bible is one book, the inspired Word of the living God." All editions of the *Scofield Reference Bible* have an introductory article, "A Panoramic View of the Bible." This article, a splendid study, is found on pages ix-xi of the introduction to the 1967 edition, and the mastery of it will be spiritually and intellectually rewarding. It says,

> *The Bible is one book.* Seven great marks attest this unity.
> (1) From Genesis the Bible bears witness to one God.

Wherever He speaks or acts He is consistent with Himself, and with the total revelation concerning Him. (2) The Bible forms one continuous story—the story of humanity in relation to God. (3) The Bible hazards the most unlikely predictions concerning the future, and, when the centuries have brought round the appointed time, records their fulfillment. (4) The Bible is a progressive unfolding of truth. Nothing is told all at once, and once for all. The law is, "first the blade, then the ear, after that the full grain." Without the possibility of collusion, often with centuries between, one writer of Scripture takes up an earlier revelation, adds to it, lays down the pen, and in due time another man moved by the Holy Spirit, and another, and another, add new details till the whole is complete. (5) From beginning to end the Bible testifies to one redemption. (6) From beginning to end the Bible has one great theme—the Person and work of the Christ. And (7) finally, these writers, some forty-four in number, writing through twenty centuries, have produced a perfect harmony of doctrine in progressive unfolding. This is, to every candid mind, the unanswerable proof of the divine inspiration of the Bible (page ix).

There are few seminary courses which will be as spiritually stimulating as the study of this "Panoramic View of the Bible." It is a three-page course in Biblical Introduction.

Facets to the truths are made so brilliantly clear in this edition that all one has to do is to thumb through the voluminous footnotes and he will find "acres of diamonds." Naturally, during our first cursory investigation we paused at Genesis 12:2, the Abrahamic Covenant. How abundantly clear is the footnote!

The Abrahamic Covenant as formed (GENESIS 12:1-4) and confirmed (GENESIS 13:14-17; 15:1-7, 18-21; 17:1-8) is in three aspects:

(1) The promise of a great nation: "I will make of thee a great nation" (GENESIS 12:2). This had primary reference to Israel, the descendants of Jacob, to whom the everlasting possession of the land is promised (GENESIS 17:8), to whom the everlasting covenant is given (GENESIS 17:7), and to

whom God said, "I will be their God" (GENESIS 17:8). Abraham was also promised that he would father other nations (cp. GENESIS 17:6, 20), principally fulfilled through Ishmael and Esau.

(2) Four personal promises are given to Abraham: (a) to be the father of numerous descendants (GENESIS 17:6). (b) To receive personal blessing, "I will bless thee," fulfilled in two ways: temporally (GENESIS 13:14-15, 17; 15:18; 24:34-35); and spiritually (GENESIS 15:6; JOHN 8:56). (c) To receive personal honor, "and make thy name great" (GENESIS 12:2), fulfilled in recognition by all who honor the Bible. And (d) to be the channel of blessing, "And thou shalt be a blessing" (GENESIS 12:2), fulfilled: in blessings to others through his seed, Israel, who became the instruments of divine revelation; through Abraham as an example of pious faith (ROMANS 4:1-22); and preeminently through Christ, Abraham's Seed (GALATIANS 3:16).

(3) Promises to the Gentiles. (a) "I will bless them that bless thee" (GENESIS 12:3). Those who honor Abraham will be blessed. (b) "And curse him that curseth thee" (GENESIS 12:3). This was a warning literally fulfilled in the history of Israel's persecutions. It has invariably fared ill with the people who have persecuted the Jew—well with those who have protected him. For a nation to commit the sin of anti-Semitism brings inevitable judgment. The future will still more remarkably prove this principle (DEUTERONOMY 30:7; ISAIAH 14:1-2; JOEL 3:1-8; MICAH 5:7-9; HAGGAI 2:22; ZECHARIAH 14:1-3; MATTHEW 25:40, 45). (c) "In thee shall all the families of the earth be blessed" (GENESIS 12:3). This is the great evangelic promise fulfilled in Abraham's Seed, Christ, and in all the spiritual seed of Abraham who, like Abraham, are justified by faith (ROMANS 4:3; GALATIANS 3:6-9, 16, 29; cp. JOHN 8:56-58). It gives added revelation and confirmation of the promise of the Adamic Covenant concerning the Seed of the woman (GENESIS 3:15).

The Abrahamic Covenant reveals the sovereign purpose of God to fulfill through Abraham His program for Israel, and to provide in Christ the Saviour for all who believe. The ultimate fulfillment is made to rest upon the divine promise and the power of God rather than upon human faithfulness (*New Scofield Reference Bible*, pages 19, 20).

As a missionary to the Jews the author can only exclaim, "Thank God!" This epitome of the Abrahamic Covenant is just one of the hundreds of footnotes that not only clarify the teachings of the Scriptures, but also courageously affirm the historic and prophetic validity of the Abrahamic Covenant. It is expected that this *New Scofield Reference* edition will be definitive in the basic theology of fundamental Protestantism. Where else in all conservative theological literature will one find the unequivocal statements, "For a nation to commit the sin of anti-Semitism brings inevitable judgment. The future will still more remarkably prove this principle?" This statement alone should completely answer the canard that fundamentalist Protestantism is anti-Semitic!

In fact, the more one studies the annotations, the more prone he is to become excited (please read the note on Romans 11:1). One might even think that he is more interested in the footnotes than the Word of God itself. This is, of course, not true; there is no substitute for the study of God's Word itself, entirely apart from any man-made commentary. Even in the printed text the publishers of the *New Scofield Reference Bible* have made the reading of the Scriptures easier and more pleasurable. The printing and layout of each page are superb; the type is easy to read. All teachers of the Word, especially missionaries to the Jews, will be delighted in the fact that the publishers retained the reverent, sublime text of the *Authorized King James Version*, but with certain word changes. These changes clarify the Scriptures, and are necessary because "some English words have become obsolete or archaic; others have altered and, in some instances, even reversed their meanings; and some have taken different forms. For example, "bakemeats" is obsolete, as is "botch" in its meaning of "a boil;" "minish" is archaic, as is "ouch" meaning "setting," etc. (introduction, pp. v, vi). With these word changes, the student will no longer have to interrupt his reading of the Scriptures with explanations. The reading of the Word itself will be self-explanatory.

We have mentioned that there is no substitute for the study of

God's Word itself, apart from man's word. This is true, but it can
be dangerous. Peter tells us that "no prophecy of the Scripture is
of any private interpretation" (II PETER 1:20). At this verse there
is a short succinct footnote in the new edition, "Any private interpretation might read 'its own interpretation'; i.e. not isolated from
what the Scripture states elsewhere."

Also, there is no substitute for studying the Scriptures methodi-
cally; we must compare Scripture with Scripture, and here the new
edition has given the Bible student an aid of inestimable value. To
this writer, the Subject Chain References are the most important
and useful feature of the new edition. Suppose, for example, a
missionary plans to teach the subject of "Sacrifice." On pages
1378 and 1379 there is an "Index to Subject Chain References."
There one will find the word Sacrifice (of Christ, prophetic, typical) followed by the reference Genesis 3:15. This is the first
allusion in the Scriptures to this doctrine, "thou shalt bruise his
heel." There is a reference letter on the word "bruise" which will
lead one to the center column references. This in turn leads to
Genesis 4:4, and then through the entire Bible, where every clear
reference or allusion to this doctrine is listed. At each listing, he
will find at least three references: one, to the first mention of the
doctrine; two, to the next reference in the Scriptures where it is
found; and finally, a reference followed by the word *note*. This
will refer to the place where there is a summary footnote. In this
particular illustration, it will be found at Hebrews 10:18, where
there is an excellent summary of this doctrine.

It is easy to see what an untold source of material this chain
subject reference will give not only to the missionary to the Jews,
but also to preachers, teachers, and all servants of the Lord.

On pages 1380 through 1387 there is a list of well over a
thousand annotations (usually footnote summaries). What a
wealth of material for the servant of the Lord! For instance, under
Types of Christ, one will find the following (and remember, this is
an annotation at each reference):

Aaron	Exodus 28:1
Aaron's rod	Numbers 17:8
Abel's sacrifice	Genesis 4:4
Altar of incense	Exodus 30:1

Burnt offering	Leviticus 1:3
Coats of skins	Genesis 3:21
Fine linen	Exodus 26:1
Isaac	Genesis 21:3 (2) 22:9
Jonah	Page 941 Introduction
Joshua	Joshua 1:1 (1)
Lampstand	Exodus 25:31
Laver	Exodus 30:18
Manna	Exodus 16:35
Meal offering	Leviticus 2:1
Melchizedek	Genesis 14:18 (4) Heb. 5:6
Moses	Exodus 2:2
Passover	Exodus 12:11; Lev. 23:5
Peace offering	Leviticus 3:1
Red heifer	Numbers 19:2
Sacrifice of the Old Testament	Leviticus 16:5
Shewbread	Exodus 25:30
Sin offering	Leviticus 4:3
Sweet Savor Offerings	Leviticus 1:9
Tabernacle, boards of	Exodus 26:15
Tabernacle, contents of	Exodus 25:9
Veil, the inner	Exodus 26:31

One can readily see the value of this edition of the Scriptures to the cause of Israel. Use it, study it, and distribute it.

VIII

A Psalm for Today

Frank E. Gaebelein

Our subject is "A Psalm for Today." The psalm to which I ask your attention is the second, and I begin by quoting it.

> Why do the nations rage, and the peoples imagine a vain thing? The kings of the earth set themselves, and the rulers take counsel together, against the Lord, and against his anointed, saying, Let us break their bands asunder, and cast away their cords from us.
>
> He that sitteth in the heavens shall laugh; the Lord shall have them in derision. Then shall he speak unto them in his wrath, and vex them in his sore displeasure. Yet have I set my king upon my holy hill of Zion.
>
> I will declare the decree: The Lord hath said unto me, Thou art my Son; this day have I begotten thee. Ask of me, and I shall give thee the nations for thine inheritance, and the uttermost parts of the earth for thy possession. Thou shalt break them with a rod of iron; thou shalt dash them in pieces like a potter's vessel.
>
> Be wise now, therefore, O ye kings; be instructed, ye judges of the earth. Serve the Lord with fear, and rejoice with trembling. Kiss the Son, lest he be angry, and ye perish from the way, when his wrath is kindled but a little. Blessed are all they that put their trust in him.

"Why?" "Why do the nations rage?" So the psalm begins like a cry in the night. "Why?" No thoughtful person can fail to ask that question. In these turbulent times, people everywhere, including multitudes behind the iron and bamboo curtains, as well as others in the free world and among the neutral nations, have been holding their breath, wondering what is coming next. And thus, as crisis has followed crisis—Cuba, South Vietnam, the Israeli-Arab

war, turmoil in our cities—and each crisis leaves continuing problems, we ask, "Why? Why have things come to such a pass?"

Let us think about that question in the light of this wonderful
psalm, surely one of the most dramatic in the whole Psalter. We
need to do this in order to gain a perspective from which to look
at our times, in order to have our thinking stabilized, as it were, in
the light of God's revealed plan. For this is part of our heritage as
believers.

The Bible makes it plain that nothing that is happening today is
a surprise to God. The course of world history is given us in
prophecy. Notice that I said "course," not "details" or "specific
dates." Biblical prophecy was not given to satisfy our curiosity
about the details of the future but to remind us that God is in
control of history, and that He is working out His sovereign purpose through the Lord Jesus Christ. The center of prophecy, as of
the whole of Scripture, is not the destiny of Israel, or of the
church, or of the nations, but the Person and work of Christ. As
John wrote in the Revelation (19:10), "The testimony of Jesus is
the spirit of prophecy."

In few places in the Bible is the course of the ages set forth
more concisely than in this mighty little psalm. Actually, this is
the first of a number of prophetic or, as they are usually called,
Messianic psalms. Others of similar character include Psalms 8,
16, 22, 23, 24, 40, 72, 89, and 110.

I have said that Psalm 2 is a psalm for today. Such it is,
because it gives us insight into what is happening in our times, and
also because it points to the future victory in Christ. But it was
also a psalm for the time long ago, centuries before Christ came,
when the enemies of God's people, Israel, were setting themselves
against David, the Lord's anointed. And it was especially a psalm
for the first century when Christ was here on earth and suffered
and died for us and rose from the dead—a time to which, according to Acts, it definitely refers. On their release from custody, after
the healing of the lame man at the temple gate and after Peter's
second sermon, Peter and John returned to the infant church. As
the record says (ACTS 4:23-27):

> And being let go, they went to their own company, and
> reported all that the chief priests and elders had said unto

them. And when they heard that, they lifted up their voice to God with one accord, and said, Lord, thou art God, who hast made heaven, and earth, and the sea, and all that in them is; who, by the mouth of thy servant, David, hast said, Why did the nations rage, and the peoples imagine vain things? The kings of the earth stood up, and the rulers were gathered together against the Lord, and against his Christ.

Not only then, but down through history this psalm has over and over again been one for the todays of God's people. The persecuted Christians of our day know its meaning. In a recent book, entitled *The Faith of the Russian Evangelicals*, the British writer J. C. Pollock says of the Baptists in Soviet Russia: "The words of the Second Psalm, which to a Westerner may be no more than archaic imagery or the libretto of one of Handel's most exciting arias, strike them as apt: 'Why do the nations rage?' "

The prophetic parts of Scripture that look to the future are like mountain ranges viewed from a distance. As one drives to Colorado from the East, after he crosses the Mississippi and Missouri Rivers, he comes to the great plains of Nebraska and the eastern portion of Colorado. Finally, at a distance of about a hundred miles, he begins to see on the western horizon the faint, blue line of the Rocky Mountains. As he draws nearer, they loom up—a jagged barrier against the sky. Then, as the miles pass, the foothills, middle ranges, and high peaks spotted with gleaming snow become visible. So, as history advances, the different aspects of predictive prophecy are clarified. With the movement of events, there is new and fuller verification of the great central truths of God's plan, culminating in the great summit of Christ's return, and of His answer to world problems, such as He gives us in this Second Psalm.

Did you notice, as I quoted it, that there is a great deal going on in these twelve verses? They begin with the question, "Why do the nations rage?" They end with the beatitude, "Blessed are all they that put their trust in him." In between are riots, plots, and counterplots; rebellion against God Himself and His anointed, followed by God's attitude toward this defiance; the coming reckoning with the nations at the return of the King and the establishment of His Kingdom; the call to get right with Him. The psalm is really an inspired world-view, a divine philosophy of the ages, a concise little outline of history as seen in relation to Christ, who is still God's anointed King today in this space age, as in the past. And all this in a dozen verses, totalling only about two hundred words in our English version!

In structure the psalm is made up of four stanzas of three verses each. As such, it may be likened to a great world-drama in four acts.

Act I. The Great Conspiracy (vv. 1-3)
Act II. God's Response (vv. 4-6)
Act III. The King's Declaration (vv. 7-9)
Act IV. The Summons to Submission (vv. 10-12)

Now not only are there four acts in this dramatic psalm, but there is also a succession of voices. In Act I the psalmist speaks, and his is the voice of an inspired man; in Act II God Himself speaks from heaven; in Act III the voice of God's Anointed, the Messiah, is heard, and His too is the voice of Deity; in Act IV the inspired voice of the psalmist speaks again.

But let us follow more closely the thought of the psalm, so that we may grasp something of its message for us today.

1. *The Great Conspiracy.* The first stanza, or act, begins with a question that is also a description. "Why do the nations rage and the peoples imagine a vain thing?" (v. 1) It is the very picture of disturbed humanity seething in turmoil and set on a course of futility, for the words, "imagine a vain [futile] thing" introduce the note of conspiracy so vividly described in the next two verses:

> The kings of the earth set themselves, and the rulers take counsel together, against the Lord, and against his anointed, saying, Let us break their bands asunder, and cast away their cords from us.

What is the futile thing that is imagined? It is the age-old rebellion against God and His Christ. It is the opposition of sinful man, so evident today, against divine authority. It is the determination to do away with the moral and spiritual restraints of Deity upon man—to "break their bands asunder, and cast away their cords" (v. 3), to snap the ties and obligations that bind the creature to the Creator. Moreover, this rebellion, while certainly an individual matter, is portrayed as a world-wide conspiracy; it is "the kings of the earth and the rulers [who] take counsel together."

Observe that this conspiracy of rulers and peoples against Almighty God and His Christ is a continuing thing. All through history opposition to the divine Majesty and, since the incarnation, to the Holy Son of God, has kept on. That the Lord Jesus Christ came into the world and was rejected is not a fact of the past alone. It has stamped its character upon the ages. In one way or another—through a corrupt church, through blatant atheism, through God-forgetting secularism, it has repudiated the Lord and His Anointed. Turning to modern history, we recall that in the eighteenth century, the French Revolution tried to dethrone God and substitute reason for Him. Since then the rejection of God and His Christ has continued, as in Germany with its pagan Nazism, in Soviet Russia and in Red China, where Communism shakes its fist at the Lord of heaven and earth, in the so-called Christian nations where multitudes live in a secularism that is little else than a practical atheism, where theological vagabonds are saying that "God is dead," and are promoting "the new morality" which cuts loose from the revealed morality of the Scriptures. Why? The answer is written large in this first act of the psalm which portrays the innate lawlessness and rebellion of sinful, unregenerate man against Deity Himself.

2. *God's Response.* In a bold transition, the second stanza directs our attention away from man to God. In one of the most striking statements in all Scripture, God is depicted as looking down and laughing in holy derision at the conspiracy of rebellious man. "He that sitteth in the heavens shall laugh; the Lord shall have them in derision" (v. 4). Between verses 4 and 5 there is obviously an interval, during which the living God, who is moved to laughter at the futility of the revolt of finite man against the infinite, everliving God, remains silent. "Then," says the psalmist, looking forward to the time when God shall act in judgment, "then shall he speak unto them in His wrath, and vex them in his sore displeasure" (v. 5). And now there comes the direct word of the living God, His response to the great conspiracy of rebellious humanity: "Yet have I set my king upon my holy hill of Zion" (v. 6). Though the words look forward to the coming reign of Christ

the King, implicit in them is the historical reference. For it is a fact that He who came two thousand years ago, and died outside the city wall for the sins of the whole world, was yet the King, as the inscription over the cross testified. And He is still the King, and His Kingdom, now unseen but spiritually real in the hearts of believers, will surely come outwardly at His return in glory and judgment. For the kingdom petition in the most-prayed of all prayers, "Thy kingdom come . . . on earth as it is in heaven," will one day be a reality when Christ returns to reign in Zion during the Kingdom age. What this will mean is shown us in the next act of this great drama.

3. *The King's Declaration.* "The answer to the problem of history," said Arnold Toynbee, the distinguished historian, "is the answer to the problem of evil." The third act of the cosmic drama portrayed in this Second Psalm brings this answer into focus through direct quotation. It is the Messiah, Christ the King, who speaks, reporting what God said to Him. "I will declare the decree" (v. 7a). And what is that decree of the living God? Just this: "The Lord hath said unto me, Thou art my Son; this day have I begotten thee" (7b). Think of it! In this third stanza of the psalm, we are enabled—let it be said reverently—to listen to God's declaration of the crucial part His Son is to have in the final settlement of the great conspiracy. But what is the meaning of the words, "this day have I begotten thee"? The reference is not, as would seem apparent, to the Virgin Birth, but primarily to the Resurrection. As Paul said of Christ in the prologue to the Epistle to the Romans, Christ was "declared to be the Son of God with power . . . by the resurrection from the dead" (ROMANS 1:4). That this is the way in which Paul understood Psalm 2:7 is clear from his quotation of it in his sermon at Antioch in Pisidia, where, in a context dealing with the Resurrection, he says, "God hath fulfilled the same unto us their children, in that he hath raised up Jesus again; as it is also written in the second psalm, Thou art my Son, this day have I begotten thee" (ACTS 13:33).

There follows a great invitation from the Father to the Son, who needs only ask to receive absolute world rule: "Ask of me, and I shall give thee the nations for thine inheritance" (v. 8). This looks forward to the ultimate transfer of power, when Christ shall reign in His Kingdom. Meanwhile we are still in the age when, as the next stanza implies, it is yet possible for men and nations to repent before the coming time of wrath and judgment.

In the Apocalypse there is one of the greatest paradoxical phrases in Scripture—"The wrath of the lamb" (REVELATION 6:16). Twenty-seven times (more than in any other portion of the Bible) our Lord is referred to in Revelation as the Lamb. The figure points to Christ in humiliation, who on the Cross voluntarily made "a full, sufficient, and perfect sacrifice, oblation, and satisfaction for the sins of the whole world." But the word as used in Revelation also has wider implications, as the Lamb is seen in the midst of the throne of the universe (REVELATION 5:6), and as He is declared "worthy . . . to receive power, and riches, and wisdom, and strength, and honor, and glory, and blessing" (v. 12). Then the figure darkens, and in the next chapter (6:16) there comes the dread phrase "the wrath of the Lamb."

"Thou shalt break them with a rod of iron; thou shalt dash them in pieces like a potter's vessel" (v. 9). With these drastic words, "the wrath of the Lamb" is portrayed. They look forward to the future time of reckoning at Armaggedon, when the King with the armies of heaven will "smite the nations: and he shall rule them with a rod of iron: and he treadeth the winepress of the fierceness and wrath of Almighty God" (REVELATION 19:15). Thus verse 9 opens a window upon "the awful unfolding scene" of the future, to use a phrase of Winston Churchill's.

Let us pause to consider the sobering fact that nowhere in Scripture do we have any warrant for assuming, as the modern mind tacitly does, that God will put up indefinitely with the rebellion of men and nations against Him. There *is* coming a day of reckoning, when the age of grace will have passed, and when the rebellion will be put down once and for all.

In the meantime, the door is open, as the last stanza of the psalm shows us.

4. *The Summons to Submission.* Since the rapture of the Church is a distinctively New Testament revelation, there is no mention of it in this psalm. But the option open to men before the culmination of world history in Christ to be reconciled to Him is set forth in poetic imagery in the final act of the great drama of Psalm 2. The call is not only for the earthly rulers to have the wisdom to recognize and serve the Son in fearful yet joyful humil-

ity—"Be wise now therefore, O ye kings; be instructed, ye judges
of the earth" (v. 10); it is also to submit to Him: "Kiss the Son
. . ." (v. 12a). This expression is an orientalism signifying submission and, while the precise meaning of the Hebrew has been ques-
tioned, the basic thought of obeisance to the Messiah is evident.
Reverence and worship are due the Son and men had better bow
in humility before Him, while there is yet time.

Following this final plea to the rebellious rulers, the psalm ends
with a beatitude: "Blessed are all they that put their trust in thee"
(v. 12b). And so this drama of the ages ends on a personal
invitation to all people everywhere to put their trust in Christ, the
Son of the living God.

What, finally, is the center of this powerful little psalm? Is it
conspiracies and tumults, nations and judgments? No, all these are
in the psalm, but they are not its center. We must ask another
question—namely, who is the center of these four great stanzas?
Is it an earthly king or dictator? No. The answer is plain. The
center of the psalm is a divine Person, the Son of God whom,
despite rejection by the world, God exalts and will ultimately
enthrone as King. He only is set forth in this psalm as the culmination of history.

Yes, "Blessed [happy] are all they that put their trust [take
refuge] in him." It is all very well to know the facts of prophecy;
but prophecy is not like some kind of biblical Cinerama, a specta-
cle we have the privilege of watching while remaining uncommit-
ted and uninvolved. Always there is the personal question: What
about our faith, our trust in Him who is the Center of prophecy?

We miss the most searching application of this psalm for today,
if we fail to see its relation to us. For we too are part of the great
conspiracy. Because we are sinners by nature and by fact, we too
have had our share of complicity in rebellion against God. Therefore, we too must know what it means to "kiss the Son," to be
sure of our peace with Him through repentance and faith in His
redeeming work, to know that our sins are forgiven through the
blood of His Cross.

Does the final beatitude of this psalm apply to you? Have you
put your trust in Christ? Is He who is the center of history the
center of your life?

IX

The Prophet Who Spoke
in an Age of Crisis

Frank E. Gaebelein

One of the problems of many Christians in their use of the Bible is that of habituation to the familiar. They know the four Gospels and Acts; they know the great Epistles; they are familiar with the well-known Psalms and some of the leading historical passages in the Old Testament. And if they have a special interest in prophecy, they are acquainted with certain key sections of the prophetical books. Yet is it not true that, when it comes to first-hand knowledge of the Word of God, there are parts of the book that are almost unknown to them? And somehow they are content to have it so.

Perhaps you may have seen in some museum, or as an illustration in an historical work, an old map, dating, say, back to the sixteenth or seventeenth century. Such maps sometimes have great areas—the western and northern parts of this continent, the interior of Africa and of South America, marked in Latin *terra incognita*—"unknown territory." Likewise with many of us and the Bible; large areas of it remain unexplored and unknown because of preoccupation with the familiar.

Now in this message I invite you to consider one of the lesser-known portions of the prophetic Scriptures—namely, the Book of Habakkuk. I do this because its writer not only tells us about God's dealings with Israel in the crisis of his time, but also gives us abiding truth that speaks to our needs today.

In 1964 it was my privilege to participate in some World Vision pastors' conferences in West Pakistan. While I was there, one of my former students, a Pakistani, presented me with a beautiful oriental rug to take home as a gift to Mrs. Gaebelein. A rug like this has an intricate design; many figures woven in different colors make up the pattern. So prophecy has many strands, all fitting together in God's sovereign plan. And we need to remember that such strands in God's great design as Israel, the nations, the Church and its destiny are all interrelated and that they all have their ultimate unity in Jesus Christ, our Saviour and Lord, the King whose return we await.

For the basis of our thought together, let me read a few portions of Habakkuk's eloquent little book.

The burden which Habakkuk the prophet did see. O Lord, how long shall I cry, and thou wilt not hear! Even cry out unto thee of violence, and thou wilt not save! Why dost thou show me iniquity, and cause me to behold grievance? For spoiling and violence are before me; and there are those who raise up strife and contention. Therefore, the law is slacked, and judgment [justice] doth never go forth; for the wicked doth compass about the righteous; therefore, justice goeth forth perverted.

Behold among the nations, and regard, and wonder marvelously; for I will work a work in your days, which ye will not believe, though it be told you. For, lo, I raise up the Chaldeans, that bitter and hasty nation, which shall march through the breadth of the land, to possess the dwelling places that are not theirs (1:1-6).

I will stand upon my watch, and set myself upon the tower, and will watch to see what he will say unto me, and what I shall answer when I am reproved.

And the Lord answered me and said, Write the vision, and make it plain upon tables, that he may run that readeth it. For the vision is yet for an appointed time, but at the end it shall speak, and not lie; though it tarry, wait for it, because it will surely come, it will not tarry. Behold, his soul that is lifted up is not upright in him; but the just shall live by his faith (2:1-4).

A prayer of Habakkuk the prophet upon Shigionoth. O Lord, I have heard thy speech, and was afraid: O Lord, revive thy work in the midst of the years, in the midst of the years make known; in wrath remember mercy. God came from Teman, and the Holy One from Mount Paran. Selah.

His glory covered the heavens, and the earth was full of his praise. And his brightness was like the light; he had horns coming out of his hand; and there was the hiding of his power. Before him went the pestilence, and burning coals went forth at his feet. He stood, and measured the earth; he beheld, and drove asunder the nations; and the everlasting mountains were scattered, the perpetual hills did bow: his ways are everlasting (3:1-6).

When I heard, my belly trembled, my lips quivered at the voice; rottenness entered into my bones, and I trembled in myself, that I might rest in the day of trouble. . . . Although the fig tree shall not blossom, neither shall fruit be in the vines; the labor of the olive shall fail, and the fields yield no food; the flock shall be cut off from the fold, and there shall be no herd in the stalls; yet I will rejoice in the Lord, I will joy in the God of my salvation. The Lord God is my strength . . . (3:16-19a).

Habakkuk was one of the twelve minor prophets, so called. But what is a prophet in the Old Testament sense? The prophets were men whom God raised up from among His people to exercise a twofold function: that of forth-telling—i.e., declaring God's message of rebuke and judgment, encouragement, or comfort, to the people of their time; and that of fore-telling—i.e., speaking about the future and God's ultimate plan for men and nations. But whatever their message, it stood in relation to the Messiah, Christ the Lord, who is *the* key to the Scripture and *the* center of God's plan.

Such a prophet was Habakkuk. He lived in the last days of the kingdom of Judah at the end of the seventh century before Christ —i.e., about 600 B.C., or nearly 2,600 years ago. Yet he speaks to our situation today as do few other portions of the Old Testament. His was a time much like ours of disorder among the nations, of injustice and corruption. Above all, it was a time of impending judgment. In Habakkuk's day, two nations, Judah and Babylon, were involved. Now many nations are involved, and we see evil on the most widespread and gigantic scale in history.

We know little or nothing about the details of the life of this man Habakkuk. But we know much about his mind and heart. Of

all the twelve minor prophets, he is the most profound—a *major*
minor prophet, if you will.

There are three chief sections of Habakkuk's prophecy, and
they are clearly relevant to us and the problems of this time of
crisis in which we are living. They are as follows:

1. The Perplexed Prophet Who Brought His Problem to the Lord
(chapter 1)
2. The Waiting Prophet Who Received the Answer from the Lord
(chapter 2)
3. The Rejoicing Prophet Who Was Strengthened in the Lord
(chapter 3)

1. *The Perplexed Prophet Who Brought His Problem to the
Lord.* The opening verse stands as a topic sentence for the entire
prophecy. "The burden which Habakkuk the prophet did see."
The word translated "burden" means the prophetic utterance or
vision that God gave Habakkuk. Yet, as the next few verses show,
the occasion for what was revealed to him was indeed a burden or
concern that weighed heavily upon his heart. He looked at Jerusalem and saw all about him wickedness and corruption. And so
he begins a bold dialogue with God. How long, he is saying, must
he cry out to the Lord without being heard; how long must he
scream, "Violence," without anything being done about it? Why
does he have to see iniquity, exploitation, and strife going on while
God is apparently not interested in stopping them? "Therefore,"
he says, jumping to a hasty conclusion, "the law is slacked, and
judgment doth never go forth" (v. 4).

It is all very human. Habakkuk is a concerned man. He is
stirred and perplexed by the shocking evil he sees in Judah. Boldly
he complains. But, and this is the significant point, he brings his
problem directly to God.

Observe that Habakkuk was not a dispassionate, unconcerned
spectator of injustice and corruption. He had what has been
strangely lacking, in these critical times in which we are living,
among too many Bible-believing Christians—a godly sense of social justice. He took up as his personal concern the burden of what
he saw and brought it to God, whereupon God gave him the great
vision of what He would do about it.

Thus Habakkuk reminds us that God greatly uses those of His

children who, looking about them, see burdens and take them up for the Lord. There would have been no Reformation had not Luther and Calvin and the other reformers seen and taken up the burden of the Lord. Nor would the great foreign missions movement have developed had not Carey and Zinzendorf, Judson and Livingstone, Hudson Taylor and Zwemer, had a burden for the unevangelized and done something about it. The abolition of human slavery and of child labor, the founding of Christian educational institutions, all go back under God to men and women who not only saw human need, but became involved in it. My friend, what is your burden? In relation to the great needs of our day, are you just a spectator or, as God leads you, are you prayerfully involved?

Habakkuk has made his complaint. Now God answers him (vv. 5-11). And He bids the prophet to look with amazement at the nations, for He will do in Habakkuk's day a work so startling as to be unbelievable until it happens. The reference is to the Babylonians (Chaldeans) who, rising suddenly to power, did indeed bring judgment upon Judah in the prophet's own day. In dramatic words, the swift destruction they brought—an ancient blitzkrieg, if you will—is described.

To this startling revelation of what God is going to do about the wickedness of Judah, Habakkuk gives a remarkable reply. He says in effect, "Yes, Lord I understand your purpose in raising up the Chaldeans against Judah." But he says this out of a great personal hold upon God: "Art thou not from everlasting, O Lord *my* God, *mine* Holy One? [italics added] O Lord, thou hast established them for judgment, thou hast established them for correction" (v. 12). The prophet goes on to speak as an intercessor, and in doing so he reminds us that powerful intercession in behalf of others rests on our own deep personal hold upon and faith in the living God.

Once more, and again very humanly, Habakkuk complains. What he is doing is to point with horror at the ruthless evil of the Babylonians, the instruments of divine judgment, the implication being that their insatiable lust for conquest (portrayed in vv. 13-17) is worse than the sins of Judah. How can God, whose eyes are purer than to behold evil with favor, countenance their crimes (v. 13)?

2. *The Waiting Prophet Who Received the Answer from the*

Lord. Still perplexed, Habakkuk does a very wise thing. "I will,"
he says, "stand upon my watch and set me upon the tower and
will watch to see what he will say unto me . . ." (2:1). "The
tower" to which Habakkuk went represents for us any place or
any way in which we, in the perplexities and problems that come to
us all, may be alone with God. The principle is a timeless one;
when we cannot understand the ways of the Lord, then we need to
wait quietly and trustingly before Him.

The prophet was not disappointed. God spoke, and in speaking
gave him one of the greatest of all prophetic messages (vv. 2-4,
especially v. 4). First, there is the injunction, "Write the vision,
and make it plain upon tables [tablets] that he may run that
readeth it" (v. 2). The reference is to the urgency of making the
prophetic message plain, so that its purpose may be fulfilled. Contrary to the opinion of many, Biblical prophecy is not necessarily
obscure. In its major points it is clear. And it must be taught and
preached with a clarity like that of public notices alongside the
road of life that whoever reads it may run, may be motivated to be
about the service of the Lord. For, properly understood, prophecy
is a great dynamic for doing the Lord's work.

Man often feels that God's answer to human problems is de-
layed. But God is never late. "At the end it shall speak, and not
lie; though it tarry, wait for it, because it will surely come, it will
not tarry" (v.3). These words are akin to Peter's well-known
statement, ". . . one day is with the Lord as a thousand years, and
a thousand years as one day" (II PETER 3:8). God's answer,
whether it be in a prophetic vision of His truth, or in guidance in
daily problems, or in the ultimate answer to all things in Christ's
return, is always for the "appointed time."

And now comes a statement—terse and pregnant with meaning
—of surpassingly great spiritual significance. "Behold, his soul
that is lifted up is not upright in him: but the just shall live by his
faith" (2:4). The first part of this verse is a vivid picture of the
attitude of all tyranny from Nebuchadnezzar down through Hitler
to the dictatorships of our own day. The picture is that of the
swollen pride of godless, arrogant power: "his soul that is lifted
up [puffed up, ASV]" with its basic twist of crookedness and
deviousness "is not upright [not straight] in him." That is all, but
it is enough! The godless, defiant power of man bears within itself

the seeds of its own destruction. There is in these few words of Habakkuk a profound philosophy of history respecting earthly powers. As Sir George Adam Smith has put it, "Tyranny is suicide." This is the principle behind Habakkuk's words, and world history bears it out.

Even more important is the second part of this tremendous verse: "but the just shall live by his faith." By any thoughtful estimate, this is one of the half-dozen most important statements in Scripture. Here is the seed that the Holy Spirit took and, implanting it in the mind of Paul, led him to develop it in the Epistle to the Romans, that greatest of all expositions of the gospel. As the Apostle said in stating the thesis of Romans, "For I am not ashamed of the Gospel of Christ: for it is the power of God unto salvation to every one that believeth: to the Jew first, and also to the Greek. For therein is the righteousness of God revealed from faith to faith: as it is written [and where is it written? In Habakkuk 2:4], The just shall live by faith" (ROMANS 1:16, 17). Here in briefest form is the way in which man is justified in the sight of a Holy God—not by works but by faith in the finished work of Christ. This is the key that by grace unlocks for the sinner all the blessings of salvation.

One of the principles of Bible study is that when the Word of God repeats something, that which it repeats is especially important. Thus it is significant that not once but three times Habakkuk 2:4b is quoted in the New Testament. In the initial citation in Romans 1:17, the emphasis is apparently upon its justification aspect (italics added to texts): "The *just* shall live by faith." In Galatians 3:11, the stress seems to be upon life: "The just shall *live* by faith." And in Hebrews 10:38, which stands at the portal of the classic summary of the achievements of faith in the lives of God's people, the emphasis is evidently upon faith: "Now the just shall live by *faith*." If Habakkuk had written nothing else but this fourth verse of his second chapter, he would be forever remembered. For here in a single sentence he gives us in germinal form the heart of the Biblical message—namely, that the pride of man leads to death but that faith in the living God is the gateway to life.

The prophecy next turns to a series of woes in which the particular sins of the Babylonians are unmasked and drastic judgment pronounced against them (vv. 5-19). Yet in the midst of these words of doom a window is opened, as it were, and the light of the coming glory of the millennial age shines through, as the prophet declares: "For the earth shall be filled with the knowledge of the glory of the Lord, as the waters cover the sea" (v. 14). And after the pronouncement of judgment is finished, it is as if there were a pause, and then we have this solemn call to reverent silence before Him who has been speaking through his prophet: "But the Lord is in his holy temple: let all the earth keep silence before him" (v. 20).

3. *The Rejoicing Prophet Who Was Strengthened in the Lord.* The last chapter of the book, though called a prayer ("A prayer of Habakkuk the prophet upon Shigionoth," v. 1), and such it is, in its form is a psalm. The puzzling word "Shigionoth" may refer either to musical instruments or to a rhapsodic kind of song. This psalm contains some of the most lofty poetry in Scripture and describes in sublime imagery a theophany, or visible manifestation of God. It opens with the prophet saying, "O Lord, I have heard thy speech, and was afraid; O Lord, revive thy work in the midst of the years, in the midst of the years make known; in wrath remember mercy" (v. 2). Here we have Habakkuk's response to the vision given him in 2:4 and to the remainder of the second chapter. Like the other prophets to whom God spoke in their encounter with Him, the fear of the Lord has overwhelmed him. Whereupon he prays for revival, not of his people but of the Lord's work, knowing full well that judgment will be entailed in such revival but begging for mercy in the midst of wrath. From such prayer, which is concerned not with our own pattern of revival but first of all with the Lord's sovereign action in renewing His work, whatever of judgment may be entailed, we have much to learn.

There follows the theophany. Poetically, its figures of speech reflect the Lord's deliverance of His people in the exodus. Images from nature abound—e.g., "He stood, and measured the earth: he beheld, and drove asunder the nations; and the everlasting mountains were scattered, the perpetual hills did bow; his ways are everlasting" (v. 6). The entire passage conveys an overwhelming sense of the awful power of the Almighty. And in its midst is this key statement: "Thou wentest forth for the salvation of thy people, even for salvation with thine anointed," a reminder that the might of the Eternal One is directed to the deliverance of His own.

No wonder Habakkuk is reduced once more to fear and trembling; as he says, "when I heard, my belly trembled; my lips quivered at the voice; rottenness entered into my bones, and I trembled in myself" (v. 16). And out of this transcendent experience of the mighty power of God, he brings us his final message, which is that, no matter what happens, even though there be famine in the land ("although the fig tree shall not blossom, neither shall fruit be in the vines; the labor of the olive shall fail, and the fields yield no food . . ." (v. 17), "yet," he says, "I will rejoice in the Lord, I will joy in the God of my salvation. The Lord God is my strength . . ." (v. 19a).

So Habakkuk has come through his perplexity and doubt about God's dealings with rebellious Judah and wicked Babylon. He comes not merely to faith, for he had that all along, but to faith enriched by joy in the God of his salvation. He has learned the full adequacy of the Lord. Translated into terms that relate to us in our day of crisis, this means that the Lord Jesus Christ is not only necessary; He is enough. If we have Him, we have all in actual potentiality. Without Him we are abysmally poor in soul. With Him, no matter what happens, we have infinite spiritual riches. In the first century, the Church had no earthly riches or prestige, but it had Jesus. And so, as T. R. Glover said, "It must be with us as it was in the first century, Jesus or nobody." The richest church and the richest Christians are those who know who Jesus Christ really is and who, knowing Him personally, know Him best of all.

How do we know Him today in a time of crisis? God gave Habakkuk the enduring answer to that question: "The just shall live by his faith." And God reiterated that answer in the New Testament and brought out of it the gospel of His grace in His Son. Thus Habakkuk, as does the whole of Scripture, brings us face to face with Jesus Christ, our only Lord and Saviour.

X

Deborah's Prophecies

Allan A. MacRae

In this essay I would like to examine three very interesting prophecies that God made about Israel.

These prophecies were fulfilled in ways that are not immediately obvious. By examining them we can learn some facts about the nature of predictive prophecy that can be helpful in consideration of other predictions.

The predictions that I have in mind are contained in Judges 4. Let us examine the situation. Israel was being punished for its sins. The Israelites had been mightily oppressed for many years by the Canaanites, who had nine hundred chariots of iron. The time came when God was ready to deliver them. He ordered His prophetess Deborah to make three very interesting predictions.

The first of these is found in Judges 4:6-7. Deborah said to Barak, "Hath not the Lord God of Israel commanded, saying, Go and draw toward mount Tabor, and take with thee ten thousand men of the children of Naphtali and of the children of Zebulun? And I will draw unto thee to the river Kishon Sisera, the captain of Jabin's army, with his chariots and his multitude."

The second prophecy is contained in the latter part of verse 7: "and I will deliver him into thine hand."

The fulfillment of these two prophecies is described in the prose narrative of Judges 4:12-16, and presented in poetic form in the song of victory in Judges 5.

With ten thousand men the Israelites would be more than sufficient in number to cope with the force of Sisera, were it not for the fine equipment that Sisera had. With his strong horses and his nine hundred chariots of iron he would have the Israelite foot soldiers absolutely at his mercy. It was on this account that Jabin had been able to hold the much larger number of Israelites in subjection for twenty years.

The strategy involved in Deborah's request is apparent if one notes the geographical situation. Mount Tabor stands out like a watchtower. It is not the highest mountain in Palestine, but it is probably the most conspicuous. It is a distinctive mountain, with a regular shape and rather steep sides, and is so situated that it can be seen from almost any part of Palestine. If ten thousand men went up on this mountain, they would be visible from all over Palestine. Sisera's chariots of iron could not attack them on the mountain, but everyone would know they were there. Sisera would be ready to pounce upon them the minute they came down.

Among the various places where Sisera might encamp in order to be ready to annihilate Barak's force as soon as it should come down from the mountain, the most attractive was the area around the river Kishon. This was a small stream that would provide water for the men and for the horses. The land around it was quite flat, so that in the normal dry condition it was an ideal place for chariots and horses to maneuver. Sisera's force could wait in comfort for the time when Barak's men would run out of provisions and would have to come down from the mountain.

Yet there was sometimes an element of danger in camping beside the river Kishon. Once in a long time a sudden storm came. The river overflowed its banks, and the whole plain became a slimy marsh in which horses and chariots were helpless. Struggling to escape, they would sink deeper and deeper into the mire. Under these circumstances they would be an easy prey for the Israelite foot soldiers. This is exactly what happened. After Deborah and Barak had taken the army up the mountain (4:10), Deborah said one day (4:14): "Up; for this is the day in which the Lord hath delivered Sisera into thine hand: is not the Lord gone out before thee?" What she meant was quite clear to Barak. From that altitude they could see in the distance the rapidly approaching storm. Suddenly striking the Canaanites, it would reduce their forces to impotence. This is memorialized in verse 4 of chapter 5: "Lord, when thou wentest out of Seir, when thou marchedst out of the field of Edom, the earth trembled, and the heavens dropped, the clouds also dropped water." The effect of the storm is described in Judges 5:21-22: "The river of Kishon swept them away, that ancient river, the river Kishon. O my soul, thou hast trodden down strength. Then were the horsehoofs broken by the means of the pransings, the pransings of their mighty ones."

As we read these verses we can vividly see the sudden unexpected downpour; the ground quickly turned into a marsh, making it impossible for horses or chariots to move; the horses struggling to pull the chariots, and instead sinking deeper and deeper into the mire, falling over, crushing the men who were trying to pull them out, and leaving all at the mercy of the attacking Israelites.

Thus the statements of the poem, together with the account in Judges 4, clearly indicate the strategy of the battle, and delineate the way in which God enabled His people to win deliverance from the Canaanite oppressors.

However, we find that originally Barak hesitated about following Deborah's advice. Deborah had assured him that God would draw Sisera with his chariots and his multitude to the place where he would be in great danger if a sudden storm were to come. Barak doubtless hoped that Deborah was indeed speaking truly and that God had predicted this through her. He knew her to be a very wise woman. For many years she had been observing political and meteorological conditions. She was aware of the impetuous character of Sisera, and of the fact that he was likely to be overconfident and a bit careless. Yet it might be that Sisera, as the years passed, had become more cautious. Suppose that he were to go to a less convenient but safer place to make his encampment. He could wait there until the Israelites were forced by starvation to come down from the mountain. Or he could leave enough of his force there to keep watch on the men cooped up on the mountain, and could send the rest to pillage and destroy their homes and to take their families captive. In this case the men would be forced to come down and try to deliver their families, and would be an easy prey to the Canaanites. Was Deborah's judgment of Sisera's character still correct? Had God actually said that He would cause Sisera to follow this somewhat incautious procedure of encamping by the river Kishon?

Moreover, Barak thought about the second prediction. Deborah said that God would deliver the Canaanites into his hand. Barak knew what it would mean if a sudden storm should come; yet such storms were quite infrequent. Suppose the storm should fail to come. This actually happened once during the Middle Ages. An army went up Mount Tabor to draw the enemy to the river Kishon, thinking that they would have a victory precisely like Barak's. No storm came. Eventually they were forced to come down and were annihilated. Was Deborah's promise that God would deliver Sisera into his hand a direct promise from God, or was it simply that her observation of weather conditions over a period of many years led her to believe that a sudden storm would come at this time of year? Suppose the storm should fail to materialize? In that case the Israelites would be at the mercy of the Canaanites.

Deborah's Third Prediction

As Barak thought over these various possibilities, he decided that he had confidence enough in Deborah's judgment to risk his life following her orders. But he was not willing to risk his reputation. He wanted it thoroughly understood, if he undertook this course of action, that it was because of Deborah's statement and because of his belief that God had spoken through her. He was determined that it should be absolutely clear to everyone, if the plan should fail, that it had been her mistake and not his. Consequently, he said (v. 8), "If thou wilt go with me, then I will go: but if thou wilt not go with me, then I will not go."

In verse 9 we find Deborah's answer: "I will surely go with thee: notwithstanding the journey that thou takest shall not be for thine honour; for the Lord shall sell Sisera into the hand of a woman."

These words of Deborah present the third prediction in the chapter. Barak probably misunderstood. He thought that Deborah meant, "If I go with you, people will give me the credit for the victory rather than you." Barak said to himself, "If we win a great victory, there will be plenty of credit for both of us. I don't need to worry about that. If we lose, it will be Deborah's fault, and my reputation will not suffer."

However, those of us who have read the chapter know that the surface understanding of these words is not what God really meant by them. Instead they refer to the death of Sisera, under circumstances that no human being could have guessed in advance. Verse 11 tells us that Heber, the Kenite, had left the rest of the Kenites, and had pitched his tent in a region not far from the area in which Sisera would make his encampment. Later on we find that when the victory came, Sisera was not killed by the swords of the Israelites. He was not trampled upon or kicked by one of the plunging horses. We are told that all the rest were killed, and only he escaped. The direction in which he happened to run was exactly the direction in which, unknown to him, Heber, the Kenite, who was on terms of peace with the Canaanites, had recently encamped (v. 17). Deborah had no way of knowing that these things would happen. Nor did she have any human way of knowing that Heber would be away when Sisera would come, leaving Jael, his wife, in a precarious position.

Deborah had no human way of knowing what action Jael would take when she saw Sisera coming. In 1929 I was a member of a party that traveled on horseback through the back country of Palestine looking for archaeological sites. If we came to an Arab village in the morning when the men were not around, but the women were working outside, it was often difficult to get directions. The Arab women were afraid of strangers. They did not know what evil the strangers might do to them, and if they should become friendly, they did not know what effects their husbands' jealousy might produce. Often they would give us a false direction in order to get rid of us as quickly as possible.

When Jael saw Sisera running down the valley, disheveled and excited, no human being could predict what she might do. If she had seen him in time, she might have run off a distance and tried to hide. She might have tried to barricade herself in the tent in the hope that he would not stop. She might simply have fled. Or she might do as she did: attempt to protect herself by deception. She went out and spoke to him in a friendly way. When she brought him into the tent, she was in greater danger than before. If her husband should return and find a strange man in the tent, he would probably kill them both. Hoping that her husband would not come back before she finished, she speedily gave him a drink that would make it easy for him to fall asleep, and then killed him.

This is not related in the Bible as an example of a godly woman, but is simply an account of what a fearful Kenite woman did to preserve her honor. The point is that Deborah's prediction was precisely and exactly fulfilled in a way that no human being could possibly have predicted.

I have called the other two predictions "organic predictions," since they were prophecies of the way in which God would deliver His people. I call this one an "inorganic prediction."

What would happen to Sisera was not particularly important for the deliverance of the Israelites. Once his entire army was gone he might have returned home in disgrace. He might have been killed by the Israelites. He might have been kicked by one of the plunging horses. His own fate was not important when his army and his chariots were gone. It was not important that it was a woman who killed him, rather than a man. It did not contribute to the accomplishment of God's work. It is not an organic prediction. It is an inorganic prediction. It is like a sign or seal pointing to the fact that God had predicted things that no human being could possibly have accurately guessed. With careful study of geographical and climatic conditions, and observation of Sisera's activities and character over a long period of years, one might have made a good guess as to what Sisera would do, and as to the fact that a sudden storm might come at this period of the year, and in such a case one could easily predict what the result would be. Someone might easily ask, "Was it God who gave the victory, or was it clever thinking on the part of Deborah?"

The Meaning of Dunkirk

In early 1940, a large British force was in France fighting against the Germans. The collapse of the Belgian army enabled the Germans to enter France with irresistible power. Great numbers of British troops were at their mercy. The Nazi radio jubilantly proclaimed that within a few days all these British soldiers would be safely penned behind barbed wire. All over England the churches were thronged as people prayed that God would deliver their armies. The great mass of British soldiers were crowded around the French port of Dunkirk, with the German force slowly but inexorably closing in on them.

Ordinarily, the English Channel is one of the roughest bodies of water in the world. I shall never forget how in 1911 my father and I crossed the English Channel from Newhaven to Dieppe. As a young boy I enjoyed the winds and the waves, and for the first five minutes I walked gleefully around the deck. By the sixth minute I was rushing into the cabin, looking for a place to lie down. For the remaining hours of the voyage I lay on one berth and my father on another near me, neither of us caring whether we lived or died, and rather hoping for the latter fate. It was the most uncomfortable day that I have ever spent.

This seems to be the normal condition of the English Channel. If it were like this, only sizable boats could be of any help in trying to rescue the British soldiers. However, for a period of several days after the invasion of France the Channel was unusually calm. People in England who had boats, even small ones, dashed across the channel to Dunkirk and filled their boats with British soldiers.

During the days of the evacuation, the sky was heavily overcast with clouds. Radar was not developed to any extent at that time. The German planes could fly above the clouds, but had no way of knowing just where the boats were, or where hundreds of thousands of British soldiers were waiting crowded together on various docks. If the weather had been clear, it would have been easy to drop a few bombs and destroy the soldiers on the docks or even the docks themselves, thus making it absolutely impossible to rescue any sizable number of the soldiers. Before the clouds lifted, great numbers of British soldiers were safely back in England. All the nation joined in a great expression of praise to God for the marvelous deliverance He had given.

Yet three years later the situation was entirely different. Most English accounts of the battle had no word of thankfulness to God for the climatic conditions that played so great a part in the deliverance. Nothing was said about the great volume of prayer that had gone up to God and how it had been answered. All that was talked about was the great valor and skill of the Royal Air Force, which was said to have driven back the German force and made the victory possible, and the great loyalty and energy of the English sailors who had rescued the endangered soldiers. Was the weather an accident, or did God actually answer prayer?

During my third year in college I became acquainted with a young woman whose father had been an earnest Christian minister. She herself, however, had lost all faith in Christianity, and had adopted an entirely materialistic viewpoint. She told me that she was then living with an aunt with views similar to her own. She told me how one day during the previous summer her aunt had taken her to town to do some shopping. As they entered the streets of Pasadena, they found it difficult to find a parking place. Then they came to a place where there was ample room, but a bicycle was parked right in the middle of it. The aunt asked her to move the bicycle to the end of the space so that the car could be parked. She said that as she started to move the bicycle she tripped and her foot caught. She fell over, and her leg was broken. At that moment, she said, there was not a single bed available in the Pasadena hospital. If she had entered the hospital at that instant, they would have turned her away because no bed was available, and there was no prospect of any becoming available in the near future. However, between the time when she was lifted into her aunt's car and the time when her aunt arrived at the hospital, a bed was unexpectedly vacated and there was a place to take care of her. "Now," she said, "If someone had prayed, this could have been cited as a most remarkable answer to prayer. However," she said, "no one prayed. It was just chance and accident." What can one answer in such a case? How can one prove that God actually does work in the world and accomplishes things in accordance with His will? In the case of the great victory of Deborah and Barak, believers can immediately say it was God's hand that led. It was God's power that gave the victory. God spoke through Deborah. Unbelievers can say that Deborah was a good observer of human nature and weather conditions. She knew Sisera's character. She knew a storm was likely to come at this time. She took a chance and it paid off. We believe that an organic prophecy was marvelously fulfilled, but we have no actual proof of it beyond our faith. However, fulfillment of the third prediction—the inorganic one—involved so many features that no one could possibly predict that it leaves no other possible explanation than divine foreknowledge. Thus an inorganic prophecy is a signpost pointing to the fact that God is active, that from the beginning God knows the future, that God possesses such control and such knowledge as no human being could possibly have.

The Garment and the Tomb

Let us look for a moment at two other very interesting inorganic prophecies. In all the Bible there are no greater organic prophecies than in Psalm 22 and Isaiah 53, where we read the marvelous predictions of the method God planned to use in saving all who would believe on Christ, whether of Israel or of other nations.

Psalm 22 is a picture of the feelings of Christ as He hung on the Cross. Spurgeon points out that its first phrase is similar to one of His cries on the Cross, "My God, my God, why hast thou forsaken me?" And that its last word, "done," is identical with His last cry on the Cross, "It is finished." Spurgeon suggested that the whole psalm was a prediction of the very words Christ would say as He hung on the Cross.

Whether it is actually a prediction of His meditation, there is no doubt that it is a prediction of His crucifixion. Crucifixion was unknown to people at the time of David, but in this psalm there is a most wonderful prediction of the details of crucifixion. However, there is one verse in the psalm that would not apply just to crucifixion in general. This is the statement in verse 18: "They part my garments among them, and cast lots upon my vesture."

The crucifixion of Christ was God's means of salvation to all who would believe on His Name. The suffering of Christ was not particularly increased by what is described in this verse. Nor was the efficacy of His death for salvation increased by it. It is an incidental inorganic prediction, pointing to the fact that this was the particular crucifixion that was predicted in the psalm, and that from the beginning God knew the end. Who could have known that in this particular crucifixion, among the articles of clothing that were divided among the soldiers there would be one that could not be evenly divided and was too valuable to tear, and that they would decide to cast lots for it? It is an incidental inorganic prediction, but a specific indication of the divine knowledge, not merely that there would be a crucifixion, but that this particular crucifixion would occur.

As Psalm 22 gives a picture of the crucifixion from the viewpoint of the One crucified, Isaiah 53 (actually Isaiah 52:13—

53:12) gives a picture of that most important event in all history as it would appear to those looking at it from the outside. It depicts the humiliation of Christ. It shows His coming exaltation. It shows the atoning effect of His death. All this is marvelously brought out in the chapter. There is, however, one statement in the chapter that is not part of the organic prediction. This is the statement in verse 9, "And he made his grave with the wicked, and with the rich in his death."

There is some disagreement as to the translation of the phrase "with the rich in his death." Some scholars think that it should be rendered "his tomb" rather than "in his death." Thus the Jewish Version of the Holy Scriptures, published since 1917 by the Jewish Publication Society, uses the rendering, "and with the rich his tomb." This makes even clearer than the translation in the King James Version its appropriateness as a prediction, hundreds of years in advance, of the sufferings of Christ and the glory that would follow.

It is hard to see any organic meaning in this phrase. The fact that He was buried in a rich man's tomb did not in any way increase His humiliation and His suffering. Nor would it be any great exaltation for Him to be buried in a rich man's tomb, nor did it add anything to the effectiveness of His death for our salvation. It is an inorganic prophecy. It is inorganic in two ways. First, it is inorganic in that it predicts an event which would not often occur, and which, while not of great importance in itself, is vital as an evidence that this is the very One who was predicted in this chapter. It shows that from the beginning God knew the end. Second, it has a further evidential purpose. If His body had been cast into a common grave of criminals, there would have been no empty tomb to show clearly to the disciples that He had actually been raised from the dead. It thus made possible the evidential aspects of the resurrection. Our salvation would be just as complete whether there was evidence or not. The wonderful work of Christ in destroying the power of Satan, and redeeming all who believe on His Name, whether Jew or Gentile, would have been just the same, whether evidence of the resurrection was available or not. But in His wonderful love and mercy God provided that the evidence of the empty tomb should be available, so that the resurrection of Christ should be clearly indicated as one of the most definitely proven facts in all history. Thus Isaiah 53:9 is an inorganic prophecy, pointing to the fact that God controls all history and knows the end from the beginning.

We can trust the prophecies. We can trust the promises of God. We can trust the Bible. Above all, let us put our faith in Him who is the principal subject of the Bible, Jesus Christ, who died to bring salvation to whosoever believes on His Name, whether Jew or Gentile.

XI

"Hath God Cast Away His People?"

Allan A. MacRae

Has God cast away His people? This is the question with which Paul begins the eleventh chapter of Romans. In fact, it is the question to which he devotes three chapters of that marvelous book.

After the first eight chapters of Romans, which contain the greatest exposition of the whole subject of human salvation that has ever been written, Paul turns aside for three chapters to consider a problem that troubled him greatly.

In the study to which he devoted so much time during the years immediately following his conversion, Paul found numerous evidences that Jesus Christ was the fulfillment of the great Messianic prophecies of the Old Testament. He saw in Him the culmination of all the work of God from the time of Abraham to his own day. As he began to preach this message and saw many people turning from darkness to light and from the power of Satan to the power of God, his heart thrilled with joy. One development, however, perplexed him greatly. As time went on he saw that while many Gentiles were coming to accept Christ, the number of Jews who turned to Jesus was becoming proportionately smaller. Thus what seemed to be the very climax of the whole history of Israel, and ought to have become the great central teaching of the nation, became the teaching of a group that was only partly composed of Jews, and increasingly composed of non-Jews. The problem perplexed Paul. He even wished that he himself might be accursed for the sake of his brethren, the children of Israel (ROMANS 9:3). As he pondered the matter, God enabled him to understand its true meaning.

We shall not at present make a detailed study of Paul's discussion of the matter. Rather we shall make a survey of the central aspects of the problem as seen in the Bible as a whole, dealing particularly with those points which illuminate the whole question and give the answer to this perplexing theme. We shall survey this material under four heads.

I. God's Promises to Abraham Are of Permanent Validity

In Genesis 12 and succeeding chapters we find the record of God's marvelous promises to Abraham. There is no suggestion in these passages that the promises were temporary in nature or would come to an end within a few centuries. God spoke positively and definitely as He predicted His continuing blessing upon Abraham's posterity.

The world as a whole had turned away from God and was trying to forget Him. In order to preserve the knowledge of the great Creator, and to prepare the way for the coming of His Son into the world, God called one man to leave the great center of civilization in Ur of the Chaldees and to go out into the unknown west, promising that through Abraham's descendants He would establish a nation whose whole life would center around its loyalty to God. God directed Abraham's attention to the things about him: to the sand that stretched interminably across the far reaches of the wilderness, and to the stars that gleamed so brightly in the heavens; and declared that these were symbols of the abiding faithfulness of God who would make of Abraham's descendants a nation too numerous to count.

Abraham is known to us preeminently as the man of faith. He believed God, and it was counted unto him for righteousness (ROMANS 4:3). God told Abraham that his posterity would be as numerous as the dust of the earth (GENESIS 13:16). As Abraham looked across the flat country through which he traveled, he had a vivid realization of the greatness of God's promise. It was easy to understand this figure of speech. The next one must have been much more difficult to comprehend.

Most people today do not know a great deal about the stars. This is due mainly to our use of artificial lighting. We scarcely notice the individual stars, and few of them stand out sharply in our minds.

A century ago, if a new comet appeared, there was great excitement. Everyone was aware of this new dot of brightness in the heavens. People would begin to ask whether it meant the approaching end of the world. Papers and magazines were filled with discussions of it. Today, if a new heavenly body appears, most people know nothing about it, unless they happen to read a small reference to it in a newspaper. We are no longer conscious of the stars, since our eyes are blanketed by the great amount of artificial light upon our streets. Our thoughts are upon other things and we hardly notice the constellations. Except for the few people who make a hobby of it, most of us cannot recognize more than two or three principal constellations.

It was quite different a century ago, and even more so in the time of Abraham. As he sat in front of his tent in the cool of the evening and looked at the stars, with no artificial light to blind his eyes or to tempt him to spend his evening reading, the constellations must have become like friends to him and to thousands of others. Many of these constellations still retain the names that people gave them thousands of years ago. Through the centuries, until recently, most people would recognize the few dozen main constellations as if they were old friends.

As one's eyes dwelled upon a particular constellation, he would note how its brightest stars form a definite pattern, and would see the fainter stars scattered around the brighter ones. The Babylonians drew star charts and made extensive observations of the passage of the planets through the constellations. Much was known about the stars in those days.

It comes as a surprise to most readers today to note what must have been obvious to almost everyone in the time of Abraham: that the actual number of stars visible to the naked eye from any one place on earth is not more than about four thousand.

Genesis 15:5 tells us that God said to Abraham: "Look now toward heaven, and tell the stars, if thou be able to number them: and he said unto him, So shall thy seed be." When he heard these words, Abraham may have been greatly puzzled. He could understand the figure of the dust. It was a tremendous illustration of the great promises that God had given about Abraham's posterity. He would have been thrilled if God had said that his posterity would shine in glory like the stars; it would have overjoyed him to think they would possess lasting qualities like the stars; he would have been greatly pleased to hear that they would have exalted positions like the stars; but he may have wondered why the stars would be used as a figure for the great number of his descendants. God said that he would be a father of many nations, but four thousand persons would hardly make up one nation, and would scarcely compare with the population of even one of the cities that Abraham had passed on his journey through Mesopotamia.

Abraham was acutely conscious of the representation of the promised posterity as being as numerous as the grains of dust. When God said the same thing about the stars, Abraham had to take it on faith, trusting that the figure that God had used must be a true one, even though he could not see how this could be so. The very next verse says that Abraham believed in the Lord and He counted it to him for righteousness.

More than a thousand years passed, and Ptolemy wrote his great book in which the stars were listed and catalogued. Any scholar reading Ptolemy's work would know about how many stars there were. Surely, if one of these intellectuals had happened to see the Book of Genesis and read the statement to Abraham in which the number of the stars was used as a figure for a tremendous multitude, he would have been inclined to hoot with derision. By this time knowledge of the great culture of Babylonia had largely disappeared. The learned man would probably have said: "What ignorant people lived in those days, to write a book that would use the number of the stars as a figure for an innumerable multitude!"

More than fourteen hundred additional years passed before the answer to the problem came. Then a Dutch technician put two lenses together and produced a telescope, and Galileo in Italy used the telescope to examine the stars. To his surprise he saw that in addition to the four thousand stars visible to the naked eye, the telescope revealed the presence of thousands of additional ones. As telescopes were improved, more and more stars became visible, until today it is known that the number of stars in the heavens is actually far greater than the number of grains of sand on the entire globe. The figure that in the light of the knowledge of Abraham's day seemed a poor one for an innumerable posterity, is now easily seen to be even better for the purpose than the figure of the grains of sand.

God's statements are not always crystal clear to us, because often they contain hidden within them a knowledge of future events or of scientific realities that the people of any particular age may not yet know. God knows all things, and we can safely trust every statement in His Word. We must be careful not to read into it anything that is not really there, but if we examine its statements carefully we find that everything that God has said, as far as we can understand it, is entirely dependable and true. What we do not understand we can safely accept in trust, knowing that some day we shall have further knowledge and be able to see how accurate every statement of God's Word is.

Another important feature of the promises to Abraham and to his immediate descendants is the promise that his seed would be a blessing to all the nations of the earth. Superficial knowledge of Hebrew has led liberal scholars in our day to reinterpret the statement as simply meaning that people would use Abraham as an example of a happy life. Careful study of the Hebrew forms, however, shows this interpretation to be quite unwarranted. The Greek translation made two centuries before the time of Christ was not in error when it translated the promise as meaning that all the nations of the earth would be blessed through Abraham's seed. Jesus said, "Your father Abraham rejoiced to see my day: and he saw it, and was glad" (JOHN 8:56).

God's first promise to Abraham contained another interesting and important statement: "I will bless them that bless thee, and curse him that curseth thee" (GENESIS 12:3). This divine promise is not limited in time. It is stated categorically and permanently. Even though Israel should fall into sin, and should seem no longer to be a recipient of God's blessing, it would still be true that God has promised that those who bring blessing to His earthly people will themselves be blessed, while those who curse His earthly people will themselves suffer the results of God's displeasure. All history is full of examples of this fact. Anti-Semitism is never justified, and never can receive God's approbation. The fate of the nations that have injured Israel is a terrible warning that God never goes back on His promises. From Haman to Hitler, history shows how dangerous it is to hate His chosen people.

II. Israel's Sin Cannot Destroy God's Promises

Isaiah faced the same problem that Paul did, but in a different situation. In that portion of his book where he looked forward to God's deliverance from exile, and then beyond that to the still more wonderful deliverance from the penalty of sin that is to be accomplished through the Suffering Servant of Isaiah 53, he faced the pessimism of those who could see no hope for the future of Israel. Isaiah 50 begins with a rhetorical question: "Thus saith the Lord, Where is the bill of your mother's divorcement, whom I have put away? or which of my creditors is it to whom I have sold you?" By this rhetorical question Isaiah declares that God has not put Israel permanently aside. He insists that its difficulties and miseries are the result of its sin, but that even so God's promises are permanent and unbreakable. The verse continues with the words, "Behold, for your iniquities have ye sold yourselves. . . ." Many other passages in this wonderful section of Isaiah stress the fact that even though Israel sins and hence must be punished, yet after the punishment God's blessing remains, and He will fulfill His wonderful promises.

Leviticus 26 and Deuteronomy 28 are two of the most beautiful and at the same time two of the most terrible chapters in the whole Bible. The first part of each of these chapters describes the marvelous blessings that God will give His people if they keep His commandments, and includes some of the most beautiful statements of divine blessing that have ever been written. However, the latter part of each of the chapters contains some of the most terrible statements that ever have been written, as they portray the misery and suffering that will come upon the people if they turn away from God. If Israel forsakes her Lord, the very forces of nature will conspire to bring her misery. Yet Leviticus 26 ends with the assurances of verses 44-45:

> And yet for all that, when they be in the land of their enemies, I will not cast them away, neither will I abhor them, to destroy them utterly, and to break my covenant with them: for I am the Lord their God. But I will for their sakes remember the covenant of their ancestors, whom I brought

forth out of the land of Egypt in the sight of the heathen, that I might be their God: I am the Lord.

The terrible statements in the latter part of these two chapters have been fulfilled in the wide dispersion of persecuted Israel through the centuries. The sufferings that Israel has undergone would have completely destroyed almost any other nation, but as Isaiah so clearly pointed out, God's promises cannot be destroyed, even by man's sin. God has not cast away His people. His promises will be fulfilled.

Jeremiah expresses the faithfulness of God toward His earthly people very vividly in chapter 31:35-37:

Thus saith the Lord, which giveth the sun for a light by day, and the ordinances of the moon and of the stars for a light by night, which divideth the sea when the waves thereof roar; The Lord of hosts is his name: If those ordinances depart from before me, saith the Lord, then the seed of Israel also shall cease from being a nation before me for ever. Thus saith the Lord; If heaven above can be measured, and the foundations of the earth searched out beneath, I will also cast off all the seed of Israel for all that they have done, saith the Lord.

III. Even the Apparent Casting-off of Israel Has a Divine Purpose

Particularly in Isaiah and in Romans we find depicted an important aspect for understanding God's dealings with Israel. Israel is to be punished for its sin, but even through this punishment the divine plan of God is to be advanced. Even through their troubles blessing is to come to the world.

In the thirtieth chapter of Isaiah the prophet declares the certainty of God's judgments to an unrepentant people. Verses 15-17 strikingly portray the divine confrontation with the arrogant leaders of Israel. In verse 15 God tells how He had promised to deliver the nation if they would but trust Him. He says, "In returning and rest shall ye be saved; in quietness and in confidence shall be your strength;" but He gives their answer: "and ye would not." This answer is elaborated in verse 16: "But ye said, No; for we will flee upon horses." God answers: "therefore shall ye flee."

They continue: "We will ride upon the swift." God replies: "therefore shall they that pursue you be swift." Man in his pride and haughtiness cannot successfully oppose the will of God. God continues: "One thousand shall flee at the rebuke of one; at the rebuke of five shall ye flee: till ye be left as a beacon upon the top of a mountain, and as an ensign on a hill."

Note the unexpected and interesting twist at the end of this denunciation. What an unusual picture of defeat! What is left is not a few fragments lying on the ground. It is not said that the wind will carry them away, so that no trace will be left. They are to be like a beacon on the top of a mountain and an ensign on a hill. Even in suffering and punishment Israel is to be a witness to God's power and to the certainty of His purposes.

It is said that Frederick the Great, the cynical Prussian militarist who delighted in the conversation of Voltaire and other caustic despisers of Christianity, once turned to his court chaplain and brusquely said, "Give me, in a word, a valid argument for Christianity," and that the chaplain immediately replied, "The Jews." Here is a factual argument that is undeniable. The great powers and lesser peoples of antiquity have all disappeared. When other ancient nations have been destroyed, their people have either completely died out or have disappeared. But through the ages the Jews have remained a distinct group, scattered here and there, often widely criticized, persecuted, suffering, yet maintaining their identity. They are a beacon on the top of a mountain and an ensign on a hill, something that cannot be overlooked or disregarded, pointing to the fact that God's Word is true, that the prophecies in His Word, both of blessing and of disaster, are sure to be fulfilled, and that the declarations of the Bible about Christ as the Redeemer, through whom alone salvation can come, are true.

From a somewhat different angle Paul points out in Romans 11 how the apparent casting-off of Israel has a divine purpose. He says in verse 11, "Have they stumbled that they should fall? God forbid: but rather through their fall salvation is come unto the Gentiles, for to provoke them to jealousy."

In the succeeding verses Paul uses the figure of an olive tree to represent the center of God's witness and blessing. He represents Israel not as cast aside, but as being in part dropped out from the center of this manifestation of God's goodness. He says in verses 17-18, "If some of the branches be broken off, and thou, being a wild olive tree, wert graffed in among them, and with them partakest of the root and fatness of the olive tree; Boast not against the branches. But if thou boast, thou bearest not the root, but the root thee." Paul shows that the casting aside for a time of some of the natural branches was indeed a punishment for Israel's sin and error. He says in verse 20, "Because of unbelief they were broken off, and thou standest by faith. Be not high-minded, but fear." Paul declares that God's purpose in the temporary casting aside of Israel is to bring blessing to the world. He says in verse 15: "If the casting away of them be the reconciling of the world, what shall the receiving of them be, but life from the dead?" Thus Paul points out that this is not a permanent casting aside. Israel is eventually to be grafted back into its own olive tree (vv. 23-24). This leads us to our fourth observation regarding God's prophetic statements about Israel.

IV. Israel Is Again to Receive a Place in the Center of God's Blessing

This part of the wonderful promises of God is clearly brought out in Romans 11. We have already noted verses 15 and 23-24. Verse 26 declares, "So all Israel shall be saved."

There is to be a marvelous fulfillment of God's permanent and unbreakable promises to Abraham. Though for a long time seemingly cast aside, all Israel is eventually to be saved. They will be a nation born in a day. They will be received back into the olive tree.

As we read the prophetic statements of God's Word, we fear that there is great suffering still ahead for Israel. But we know that God's mercy will never leave them. In Isaiah 62:7 God declared that He will "make Jerusalem a praise in the earth." Verse 12 says, "And they shall call them, The holy people, The redeemed of the Lord: and thou shalt be called, Sought out, A city not forsaken." Isaiah 66:8 says, "Who hath heard such a thing? who hath seen such things? Shall the earth be made to bring forth in one day? or shall a nation be born at once? for as soon as Zion travailed, she brought forth her children."

After the rapture of the church, God has important purposes for Israel. She is to go through great suffering. She is to bear a great witness, and in the end she is to be as a nation born in a day. They will look upon Him whom they have pierced and will turn to Him with all their hearts. In the millennium Israel will have a vital part, and will continue to be the recipient of God's blessing.

No wonder that Paul, in the beginning of Romans 11, after he asked the question, "Hath God cast away his people?" broke out into the strong exclamation, "God forbid." God's promises can never be destroyed. Praise God for the way He has used the seed of Abraham through the years.

In every generation there have been Jews who have turned to Christ. Many of them have become great Christian leaders. In our day many individual Jews are turning to Christ. As we see a neighbor or a friend and think of what terrible misery may be ahead if he goes into the tribulation period without having accepted Christ as Saviour, let us be active and constant in our endeavor to win him to the Lord. Even though Israel is to be a nation born in a day, blessed indeed are those who see their Messiah now and turn to Him. Let us be active in bringing them the knowledge of the Messiah. Let us pray that God will lead many individual Jews today to accept Christ. Let us also praise Him for the plan He has revealed, that all Israel is to be in the future a recipient of His blessing and an instrument of His grace.

XII

The Power Struggle of the End Time

Clarence E. Mason, Jr.

I. Prelude and Explanation

For as long as I can remember, I have known and rejoiced in the truths related to the future purpose of God with Israel and the nations, the unique place of the church in the economy of God, and the great fact of our Lord's second advent. My father and mother came into a knowledge of these things at the turn of the century, and the entrance of this line of Scripture truth revolutionized their Christian lives, leading to fervent, lifelong Bible study with a library that would do credit to an average pastor. The truth of the imminent coming of Christ led them to an intense desire for a holy life, earnest witness to the unsaved, and dedicated devotion to the cause of missions in calling out a people for His name from among the nations.

As a result, some of the great teachers in biblical and prophetic study were household names, especially since quite a number were guests in our home. I was weaned on the *Scofield Reference Bible* (1909 edition) and Larkin's charts, with liberal doses of Gaebelein, Gray, Torrey, Blackstone, and others. I was taken to Bible conferences at a tender age. D. M. Stearns and W. H. Griffith Thomas were neighbors. Later I attended a college and seminary committed to this position, being in the first class at Dallas Seminary and privileged to sit under such men as Lewis Sperry Chafer, H. A. Ironside, A. C. Gaebelein, George Guille, B. B. Sutcliffe, and A. B. Winchester. I have been associated with Philadelphia College of Bible since 1928, and for twenty years of that time served as a pastor who believed in bringing the best American and English Bible teachers to my church. For eight years I directed the Boardwalk Bible Conference in Atlantic City, where most of the outstanding Bible teachers of that era were invited to serve.

I have recited the facts of my close association with the premillennial, dispensational, pretribulational movement to affirm that I
am and have been firmly and satisfyingly committed to the things
for which this Congress on Prophecy stands. Therefore, when in
this message I express a viewpoint that runs counter to the almost
universally held position of prophetic teachers, I want to make it
clear that I am a member of the *loyal* opposition! I am not trying
to undercut the basic unity of the position we all hold dear.
Rather, I am offering an alternate solution to one of the areas in
which I have felt our hermeneutics as a movement has been faulty.
I have found many people confused by a seeming contradiction. It
is as though two lines of prophetic exposition go down two different one-way streets which run in opposite directions, and there is
no collision because they are not on the same street. It is my
conviction that, interpretationally, they are on the same street and
should be dealt with together instead of separately.

II. Two Debatable Positions: One Antichrist
and One World Ruler

I refer to the almost universally held thesis of prophetic teachers that there is to be a world ruler, Satan's man, who will domi-
nate the whole inhabited earth. There is a collateral view that
usually goes along with it, namely, that there is a single individual
—whether one identifies him with the universal ruler in Rome or
his Jewish ally in Jerusalem—who is to be called *the* Antichrist,
despite the objection that our Lord said, "There shall arise false
Christs" and "Many false prophets shall rise" (MATTHEW 24:24,
11).

Indeed, the word "antichrist" does not occur in the New Testament in the singular except in one passage, and there it is not used
as a name but as a phrase describing an erroneous attitude or
doctrine. The passage is I John 4:3, where we read: "And this is
that spirit of antichrist, whereof ye have heard that it should
come, and even now already is it in the world." If one insists that
the passage is talking about an individual person who can be
labeled Antichrist, he must also accept the erroneous position that
the Antichrist was *already in* the world as of the first century (in
John's day).

Those who urge the theory of one certain individual Antichrist plainly expect him to be manifest after our Lord Jesus comes in the air to take His Church to heaven. Thus, although it may well be true that one superman raised up by Satan may supremely be dominated by Satan and supremely deceive men, the term "antichrist" cannot be limited to that one individual, for our Lord declared there were to be plural "false Christs . . . *many* false prophets."

In my judgment, a substantial amount of time has been wasted on the platform and in books on prophetic themes arguing *which* of the beasts of Revelation 13 is *the* Antichrist. Indeed, godly brethren have at times gotten so warm in their debate on this question of which is the Antichrist that fellowship has been cooled, if not broken.

I have no desire to raise a question which is inconsequential or which would confuse the children of God. At the same time, I wish it were possible for some interested prophetic teachers to get together and debate among themselves some of the different slants that appear in the published or spoken viewpoints of men who are essentially agreed on basics but differ on secondaries. It seems to me that a Congress on Prophecy like this is the next best thing, but I wish the former were possible. I refer to such questions as: Just what and when is Armageddon? Who or what are Gog and Magog, and when does the assault of Ezekiel 38-39 take place? Are there to be many antichrists or one supreme Antichrist? What is meant by the "drying up of the Euphrates"? Who is the king of the south?

In this message I should like to submit for your consideration the viewpoint that in the end time of the tribulation there is to be not just one great ruler (and/or sphere of authority), but *four* great spheres of political authority backed up by military might. I will submit evidence to support the view that only in the movement and attack of the armies of these four power spheres do we find room for numerous Scriptures to be explained and fulfilled; that the usually received idea of a central, universal ruler over the whole inhabited earth will not properly allow for those great tensions and movements of armies of which both Old and New Testament speak. And may I request your gracious forbearance and wise suspension of judgment until I have presented that part of the evidence for which I have space? I shall greatly appreciate your cooperation in reading me through and then searching "the Scriptures daily" to see if these things I present are so (ACTS 17:11). I shall welcome correspondence from anyone interested by what he reads in this essay.

Perhaps it would be well, first of all, to present the two lines of Biblical data that seem to collide and require some kind of adequate solution.

III. The Case for the One-World-Ruler Thesis

In Revelation 13:1-10 we read of the sinister "beast . . . out of the sea" who is commonly identified as the ruler of the revived fourth world empire, which was Rome. The revivification is based upon the statement that the "deadly wound was healed" (v. 3). History records the "death" of the Roman Empire of the West in A.D. 476 and the fall of the last remaining bastion of the Eastern Roman Empire (Constantinople) in A.D. 1453. To every intent and purpose Rome was dead and buried.

But this passage says that the deadly wound will be healed, that the empire that was Rome will be revived. The correctness of this interpretation is affirmed by Daniel 2 and Daniel 7. There, in the imagery of the colossus (ch. 2) and of the four beasts (ch. 7), it is made apparent that there is not to be a fifth *human* empire superseding the fourth. The stone which is cut out of the mountains without hands supernaturally smites the image in its final form ("ten toes"), pulverizes it, and grows into a great mountain filling the whole earth (2:34-35). Daniel 2 also includes the divine interpretation that this is the Kingdom of our Lord Jesus Christ which the God of heaven will set up on earth (vv. 44-45). Thus, if the deadly wound is healed and there is not to be a fifth empire of human origin, the revivification of the fourth empire must be the correct interpretation.

The Revelation 13 passage then goes on to say that the Roman beast will "make war with the saints and . . . overcome them; and power was given to him over all kindreds, and tongues, and nations," and that "all who dwell upon the earth shall worship him" unless their names are written in the Lamb's book of life (vv. 7-8). This seems at face value to indicate complete sovereignty over the whole earth.

IV. The Seeming Contradiction to the One-World-Ruler Thesis

However, when we turn to the Old Testament we seem to find many prophecies telling of armies marching against Palestine. In addition, our Lord Jesus Christ speaks of Jerusalem being surrounded with armies, of a crescendo of nations warring against nations until the Lord Jesus intervenes by means of His second coming in power and glory (MATTHEW 24; LUKE 21). Let us look at two or three key passages emphasizing this fact.

Turn to the prophecy of Zechariah, chapter 12. We read in verses 2 and 3:

> Behold, I will make Jerusalem a cup of trembling unto all the peoples round about, when they shall be in siege both against Judah and against Jerusalem. And in that day will I make Jerusalem a burdensome stone for all peoples: all that burden themselves with it shall be cut in pieces, though all the peoples of the earth be gathered together against it.

Again, in verse 9 of the same chapter we read: "And it shall come to pass in that day, that I will seek to destroy all the nations that come against Jerusalem."

In chapters 38 and 39 of Ezekiel we are told of a host which will come against Palestine and Jerusalem. It will be so large that when God smites the invaders upon the mountains of Israel, it will require seven months to bury the dead. Many expositors are convinced that this is the occasion, mentioned in Zechariah 14:2, when Jerusalem will be actually taken and spoiled in battle, although the successful invader is evidently in the process of withdrawal homeward, according to Ezekiel 39, when five-sixths of his large army is destroyed by God. There is almost universal agreement among prophetic scholars that this army comes from Russia and her satellites, whose ruler is known as "the king of the north" in the pattern of end-time events.

However, the north is not the only area from which assaults

against Palestine come. In the prophecy of Daniel, chapter 11, it is said that "the king of the south" shall first "push" against the man in Jerusalem, which "push" is quickly followed by the invasion of the "king of the north," who comes against the ruler in Jerusalem "like a whirlwind" (v. 40).

Further, we are informed that "tidings out of the east . . . shall trouble" the Jerusalem ruler, so that he hurries back from the south to "plant the tabernacles of his palace between the seas [Mediterranean and Dead Seas] in the glorious holy mountain [plainly Jerusalem]."

To what do those "tidings out of the east" refer? The Bible does not leave us in doubt. In Revelation 9:15 we are told of an army of two hundred million men. Associated with the announcement is the statement that the four angels binding the river Euphrates are "loosed." A parallel passage in Revelation 16:12 throws a great deal of light on the matter: "And the sixth angel poured out his vial upon the great river Euphrates; and the water thereof was dried up, that the way of the kings of the east might be prepared."

Regardless of what "the drying up of the Euphrates" means, it is clearly connected with the invasion of an army of two hundred millions of men led by the kings of the east (sunrising). This abundantly explains why "tidings out of the east" trouble the man in Jerusalem of Daniel 11.

This should be sufficient evidence to make the issue clear: namely, if there is to be a world ruler "over all kindreds and tongues and nations," how is it possible that armies are able to come at him from the south, the north, and the east? What kind of authority is unable to control his territory any better than that? Here is a ruler supposed to be in complete authority over the earth, and yet the king of the north successfully invades the land and takes the capital city of his ally in the east (the false prophet, ruler over the Jews in Jerusalem). And even more damaging to the theory is the question: How could an army of two hundred million men be raised, come all the way west against him, and presumably successfully invade that part of his territory west of the Euphrates?

I find it difficult to understand by what stretch of the imagination a man could be called a world ruler who has so little power that armies from the south, from the north, and from the east can come against him in startlingly large numbers and, judging by the language of Ezekiel 38-39, Zechariah 14, and Revelation 16, be successful in invading the land and, at least temporarily, in taking the capital city (Jerusalem) of the eastern ally of the "world ruler." The idea is completely untenable to me.

Further, since it is plainly prophesied by our Lord and others that Jerusalem will be surrounded with armies, and since we are told in the Revelation that the armies of the beast and the false prophet will be drawn up at Armageddon when our Lord descends to the earth, how can these things be if there be a universal world ruler? Does he come against himself? Does he surround himself? If not, against whom are his armies drawn up at Armageddon? Against heaven? If against heaven, why not in Jerusalem? Why go up to Armageddon? Or does anyone seriously believe, as I have heard, that a handful of repentant Jews who refuse the mark of the beast could actually mount a sort of Maccabean revolt and, barricaded in Jerusalem, successfully defy the beast and the false prophet? This taxes my credulity!

V. The Suggested Solution to the One-World-Ruler Thesis

There seems to be a plain contradiction if the Bible teaches a powerful world ruler, but also teaches invading armies from three directions, with Jerusalem surrounded and armies drawn up at Armageddon.

I have a very simple suggestion to offer that solves the whole problem for me, and I trust will commend itself to you. I feel the thing that has confused expositors is the word "world," especially when it is a translation of the Greek word *oikoumene*, which is translated "world" but means literally "the inhabited earth." There is no doubt that to an English-speaking person this means the complete globe. But the first law of hermeneutics of a language, or even translation of a language into another, is that a language means only what it meant to the people who used it in the first instance. What did the word *oikoumene* mean to the people of the first century A.D. when our New Testament was written?

Fortunately, we have a classic example. In the very familiar

story about the events leading to the birth of Jesus, as recorded in
Luke 2, we have this statement: "And it came to pass in those
days, that there went out a decree from Caesar Augustus that all
the world [*oikoumene*] should be enrolled for taxing (LUKE
2:1)."

Were the Chinese or Japanese enrolled by Augustus? Were the
Incas of South America enrolled, or the Iroquois of New York, or
even the ancestors of the Russians? Or the Ethiopians? Who were
enrolled?

Plainly we have the solution in the use the Romans made of the
word *oikoumene*. The *Roman* world was the *only* world to them.
All others were barbarians. No one else counted, because they
were not in the only world that counted, the *Roman* world. Scofield has an excellent note here. He says: "This passage is note-
worthy as defining the usual N. T. use of *oikoumene* as the sphere
of Roman rule at its greatest extent." The *New Scofield Bible* is
even more precise: "The 'world' (Gk. *oikoumene*, signifying "the
inhabited earth") throughout the N. T. has reference politically to
the Roman Empire or the Roman world."

Thus, this first-century passage in a first-century book (REVELA-
TION 13) must be understood in that light. It is "all kindred, and
tongues, and nations" in the *Roman* "world" that are involved,
that *part of the world* over which the revived fourth empire of the
west will have sovereignty. If this view be accepted, then it is
perfectly intelligible that kings of the south and the north and the
east can and will come against the Roman ruler and his ally.
Those nations are *outside* the "Roman" world, as revived. Thus,
there is no contradiction whatever.

VI. Marching Armies in the End Time

The argument above shows that, contrary to the usual concep-
tion, in the end time of the tribulation there will be *four* great
spheres of political authority backed by military might, *not just
one*. The revived fourth empire is the empire of the West, the
"United States of the Western World," composed of all that was
once Rome and that which came out of Rome, i.e., the Western
Hemisphere.

Indeed, it would appear that the very pretensions of the defiant "beast," heading the revived fourth empire (REVELATION 13:5), will arouse resentment and antagonism in the rulers of other parts of the world: south, north, and east.

At any event, Jerusalem, as the eastern capital of the fourth (western) empire, will be presided over by the ally and lieutenant of the ruler in Rome. This man is the second beast or false prophet of Revelation 13, who makes an image of the Roman ruler, desecrating the restored temple and making further sacrifice impossible (DANIEL 9:27), as in the days when Antiochus Epiphanes defiled the altar in Jerusalem by sacrificing a sow upon it. This act of the false prophet in Revelation 13 is the "abomination of desolation" spoken of by the Lord Jesus (MATTHEW 24:15), because of which horrible persecution will be the portion of those who do not go along with him.

This arrogant attitude will evidently anger those outside the Roman empire, and Jerusalem, in the providence of God, will become a mighty magnet drawing the armies of the nations to it that the Lord may destroy them (ZECHARIAH 12:2-3, 7-9). It is not insignificant that only comparatively recently have Asia and Africa become strong in political and war potential.

Using Daniel 11:40 as our starting point, we shall seek to trace and chart the movement of armies in the end time, leading up to the final destruction of the beast and the false prophet at Armageddon when our Lord Jesus returns the second time.

The four political areas of the world to be distinguished are listed below and the movement of their armies sketched on the accompanying map:

No. 1 -   *The Jewish "Wilful King" in Jerusalem* (DANIEL 11:45, labeled 1b on the chart, is allied to the Head
WEST   of Revived Fourth (*Western* or Roman) Empire (DANIEL 2:40-43; 7:7-8) whose headquarters are in Rome (labeled 1a on the chart).

No. 2 -   *The King of the South* (Africa) who "pushes at" No. 1b (DANIEL 11:40a), located in Jerusalem. No. 2
SOUTH   seems to be allied with No. 3 (DANIEL 11:43b; EZEKIEL 38:5-6), and his attack is evidently designed to draw No. 1b out of position (with his back to the north). No. 2 initially succeeds in capturing Egypt

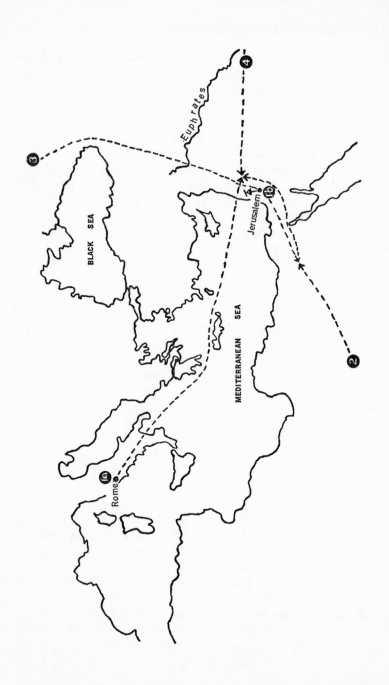

with the special help of Ethiopia and Libya (DANIEL 11:42-43; EZEKIEL 38:5).

No. 3 -   *The King of the North* (the Assyrian, Gog-Magog, i.e., Russia, etc., ISAIAH 10:24-27; 14:25; MICAH 5:5-6;
NORTH   EZEKIEL 38-39) in the meantime swoops down, while No. 1b has turned south to protect his flank against No. 2. (No. 1b is evidently soon able to neutralize the armies of No. 2, for we hear no more of No. 2.) This accomplished, No. 1b hastens back to Palestine because of unfavorable tidings out of the north and east (DANIEL 11:44), but before he can get back, the King of the North (No. 3) has already taken Jerusalem (ZECHARIAH 14:2; DANIEL 11:40b-43a; compare ZECHARIAH 12:2; 13:8-9) and started his return journey home. However, No. 3 is *smitten by God* upon the mountains of Israel (ZECHARIAH 14:3; EZEKIEL 38:21-39:4; cp. Sennacherib's destruction, ISAIAH 37:36-37) before No. 1b can counterattack him. But No. 3's invasion has laid open the eastern flank of No. 1b to attack (evidently the meaning of the Euphrates being "dried up," REVELATION 16:12).

No. 4 -   *The Kings of the East* ("Sunrising," DANIEL 11:44; REVELATION 16:12) now proceed westward with an
EAST   army of two hundred million men (REVELATION 9:16), sweeping through the eastern part of the fourth empire with great destruction (REVELATION 9:17-18). Meanwhile No. 1b hastens northward and deploys his army (now strengthened with legions from his ally in Rome, No. 1a) in the valley of Megiddo, readying for No. 4's assault.

Evidently, they (Nos. 1a and 1b and No. 4) never actually join battle at Megiddo, as it would seem that "the sign of the Son of Man" then appears in the heavens (MATTHEW 24:29-30), diverting their attention from each other and leading to further blasphemy on their part (PSALM 2:1-3). At this point the Lord Jesus Christ returns (PSALM 2:4-9), definitely smiting No. 1a and No. 1b (as told in REVELATION 19:11-21 and as alluded to in DANIEL 11:36d, 45b, with 12:1); and evidently the Lord also smites No. 4, for "Armageddon" (REVELATION 16:16) is mentioned in the same context with the kings of the east (REVELATION 16:12).

By this explanation, we understand (1) how Jerusalem will come to be attacked, (2) the part of the movement of the armies of the south, north, and east play, and (3) why the beast and false prophet have their western empire army drawn up at Armageddon at the time the Lord Jesus descends to set up His glorious earthly kingdom.

VII. Two Explanatory Notes as Postscripts

Two explanatory notes are needed to complete this study.

First: In both Daniel 11 and Ezekiel 38, Libya and Ethiopia are mentioned in such a way as to make it evident that these names are used to identify the king of the south of the end time. It should be immediately pointed out that Ethiopia was *never* conquered by Rome and thus was never in the fourth world empire. Further, only a casual glance at a map of the Roman world of the first century is necessary to make it clear that all Rome ever possessed of the great continent of Africa was the northern lip, which read from east to west as follows: Aegyptus, Cirenaica, Africa (from which later the whole continent was named, as the name of the continent of Asia was taken from the southwest province of what is now Turkey), and Mauretania. I would particularly call your attention to the fact that none of these northern fringe provinces was called Libya. Although Herodotus had no idea of the shape of the continent of Africa, his map of Africa puts Libya south of the coast, thus indicating the interior. The *National Geographic* map of the Roman Empire makes Libya the *whole* of the *interior* under the Roman lip of North Africa, except Ethiopia to the east. Evidently, therefore, the *Biblical* terms Ethiopia and Libya are to convey the idea of the whole continent excepting the Roman lip on the north coast. Confirming this, Daniel 11:42-43 indicates Egypt is attacked and its treasures taken. Thus Egypt is that part of the Roman empire the king of the south invades.

Second: The expositors have had a problem in the identification of the antecedents to the "he's" of Daniel 11:40b and the verses following. Both Gaebelein and Ironside, from whom I received the basic idea of the movement of armies, think that once the king of the north (No. 3 on the chart) comes on the scene in verse 40b, all the "he's" thereafter refer to him, and that thus he sets his tents victoriously upon the glorious holy mountain (v. 45a) and is destroyed by the Lord (v. 45b).

I find this thesis objectionable for a number of reasons. First and foremost, this interpretation does not finish the dramatic story of the "Wilful King," so strikingly begun in 11:36-39. Further, it does not make apparent why the Wilful King, after blunting the attack of No. 2 (the king of the south), would hurry back home; nor does it show why he would take his army up to Armageddon. Evidently, the king of the south is so closely allied with the king of the north that any victory of the king of the south is counted as also a victory of the king of the north (v. 43). Why then should the "he" of verse 44 be the king of the north? Why should he be disturbed about his own invasion of Palestine and conquest of Jerusalem? This would not be news to him or his ally, nor be anything to cause fear. Thus, the problem is to distinguish the "he's" of verses 40-45.

My suggested solution is to make the "he's" of verses 40b-43 refer to the king of the north both in his own activity and that of his ally, the king of the south. I then bring the story back to the Wilful King in verse 44, which explains that while he is fighting the king of the south, the king of the north has taken Jerusalem (vv. 40b-43). Hence, the Wilful King, hearing these ill tidings out of the north and hearing of the approaching march of the kings of the east toward Palestine (v. 44), furiously completes the defeat of the king of the south and swiftly moves back north to deal with the king of the north and the kings of the east. On returning to Jerusalem, he finds the king of the north has been destroyed by the Lord upon the mountains of Israel. He re-establishes his palace in Jerusalem (v. 45a), then goes to Armageddon with his Roman ally to make a stand against the kings of the east. But there he comes to his end (v. 46b), being smitten by the Lord Jesus Christ at Armageddon on His way down to the Mount of Olives. All this fits exactly with the context of Daniel 12:1 as being the end of the tribulation period.

XIII

The United States of the Western World

Clarence E. Mason, Jr.

I. The Trend Toward Western World Unity

Is it a happenstance that such titles as the above are being used on every hand in the secular press as well as in prophetic writings? I think not, for this is to be the final condition of the Western world, according to Scripture.

Not long ago the front cover of *U.S. News and World Report* carried a picture of M. Paul Reynaud of France, with large white letters emblazoned on a red background reading, "Coming—A United States of Europe." The *Saturday Review* published a convincing article by Roscoe Drummond, condensed as the lead article in the *Reader's Digest*, entitled "The United States of Europe —Hope of the West." At the time of the formation of the Common Market, *Life* carried an editorial, "Birth of Unity for Europe," whose opening words stated:

> On Capitoline Hill in Rome, nearly 2,000 years ago, Caesar's legions went forth to bring the first unified rule to Europe's warring tribes. Since the Roman Empire's fall the unification of Europe has been a dream which neither the sword of Napoleon nor Hitler could realize. But on Rome's Capitoline Hill last week six statesmen, with the peaceful stroke of a pen, took the biggest step yet made toward this dream of centuries.

If a prophetic teacher at this Congress had tried to summarize the trend in the Western world toward unification in accordance with Scripture, he could not have said it better. If men in secular circles can see these things shaping up, why is the average pulpit so silent and why are the people of God so uninformed?

In similar vein, the lead paragraph in *Time* on that occasion (Jan. 12, 1959) read:

> When the history of the 20th century is written, last week is likely to prove one of its watersheds. For in the seven days which spanned 1958 and 1959, Western Europe began to flex its economic muscles for the first time in a decade, and took its biggest step toward unity since the death of Charlemagne 1,145 years ago.

The idea of Western unity was not born yesterday. Lloyd George first used the name "United States of Europe" at the close of World War I, when he foresaw what has since been undeniably proven true: that there is no future for a divided Europe. Benjamin Franklin once said to the representatives of the struggling, divided colonies of America, "Gentlemen, if we do not hang together, we shall hang separately." Europe, facing the menace of the Russian bear, has made significant progress in the last few years toward cooperation and eventual unification.

Since this is taught in Scripture, the Bible student watches these events with great interest. We do not try to make shrewd guesses in the light of the newspaper, but first we get a firm grasp upon what Scripture prophecy says will be the ultimate outcomes, and then interpret our newspapers *by the Bible.* There is nothing in Scripture to determine which cycle of history we are in. We may swing away from the present trend, but the swing will be temporary. The next cycle will swing closer. Only God knows when the last cycle will occur, and men would be wise not to try to become prophets by stating categorically that we are at such and such a point in God's program. This dishonors Scripture, and is in direct contradiction to our Lord's warning not to set any time markers. But the Bible-taught person can certainly recognize that the trend is moving strongly toward fulfillment, even though he properly leaves the time elements with God. However, we are getting ahead of ourselves on our subject. Let us examine next

II. The Scriptural Background to Western Unity

This theme takes us back to the Book of Daniel, chapters 2 and 7. In chapter 2, we have a majestic image picturing Gentile world power as man looks upon it, with flags waving, and drums beating, and the intoxication of conquest. But in chapter 7, we see the same thing from God's viewpoint. We see succeeding world powers as savage beasts of the jungle, slashing and attacking one another and fighting to the death. This is the painful, ugly side of war of which General Sherman spoke.

The extent of the period of time which the image of Daniel 2 pictures is easily determined. God revealed it to Daniel, who informed the king, Nebuchadnezzar, that it began with him and his Babylonian Empire. "Thou, O king, art a king of kings: for the God of heaven hath given thee a kingdom. . . . Thou art this head of gold" (2:37-38). This is the beginning of that period of the world's history called by our Lord Jesus Christ "The Times of the Gentiles," since Israel had failed to rule properly for God in the theocracy. Daniel was in Babylon because of Jewish disobedience. Jerusalem and the nation were shortly to fall. This, then, is the *terminus a quo*.

The *terminus ad quem* is also plainly revealed in Daniel 2. The image is traced from the head (Babylon) down to the feet with its ten toes, when we read:

> Thou sawest till that a stone was cut out without hands, which smote the image upon his feet that were of iron and clay, and brake them to pieces. Then was the iron, the clay, the brass, the silver, and the gold broken to pieces together, and became like the chaff of the summer threshingfloors; and the wind carried them away, that no place was found for them: and the stone became a great mountain, and filled the whole earth (2:34-35).

This is interpreted as follows by verses 44-45:

> And in the days of these kings shall the God of heaven set up a kingdom which shall never be destroyed. . . . Forasmuch as thou sawest that the stone was cut out of the mountains

without hands, and that it brake in pieces the iron, the brass, the clay, the silver, and the gold; the great God hath made known to the king what shall come to pass hereafter: the dream is certain, and the interpretation thereof sure.

It is therefore apparent that the Times of the Gentiles last from the transfer of delegated power to rule from Israel to the Gentiles in the days of Nebuchadnezzar II, and that Gentile world power will continue until it is smashed by the intervention of the supernatural second coming of Jesus Christ, whose Kingdom will supersede the kingdoms of this world and "never be destroyed."

This chapter also fills us in on the major transitions of the intervening period between the start and the conclusion of the Times of the Gentiles. We should know this order of the succession of kingdoms from history, but it is significant that God proved His uniqueness as God by revealing these facts long before they occurred (ISAIAH 44:6-7; 46:9-10; contra 47:12-13).

The next two kingdoms, following Babylon (625-539 B.C.), are the "breast and arms of silver," emphasizing the duality of Medo-Persia (named in 8:20) and the "thighs of brass" (v. 32), named as Greece (8:21). The usual dates for these kingdoms are 539-331 and 331-323 B.C. respectively.

History tells us that Rome overcame the Grecian empire begun by Alexander the Great, carried on by his generals following his death, and chiefly important in Israel's history as perpetuated in the Seleucid dynasty of Syria and the Ptolemaic dynasty of Egypt. The name "Rome" is not given us in Daniel, but there can be no doubt that Rome is intended, for it was known in literature as the "iron kingdom," taking this imagery from the fact that it was first to forge weapons of this material, and because it was the nation which destroyed the only temple in Jerusalem built after the passing of Medo-Persia and Greece from the scene. The A.D. 70 destruction of the city of Jerusalem and its sanctuary are predicted in Daniel 9:26. The Roman Titus did this. Thus, Rome is the Fourth World Empire in the Times of the Gentiles.

However, despite its strength which permitted it to break in pieces and subdue opposing nations (2:40), we are told that "the kingdom shall be divided" (v. 41). It is instructive to observe that three periods of Rome, the Fourth World Empire, appear to be designated by the Scripture as follows: (1) the legs of iron; (2) the feet of iron and clay; (3) ten toes of iron and potter's clay.

FIRST PERIOD: The Two Legs of Iron (2:40)= THE ORIGINAL EMPIRE (2:33a)

While two legs suggest mobility and strength, they nevertheless indicate the inherent basic division of the empire from the beginning into East and West. And, to quote Rudyard Kipling: "East is East, and West is West, and never the twain shall meet. . . ."

Thus, the eventual division of the empire into eastern and western parts was predicated in its very constitution. The division began under Diocletian when in A.D. 286 he associated Maximian with himself; but Constantine again united the empire. Yet he paved the way for its final division later, in 364, by building the great city of "Constantine-ople" (City of Constantine) as a second Rome.

SECOND PERIOD: "Feet . . . of iron and clay" (2:41)= THE INTERVENING PERIOD (2:33b)

The eventual division of the empire into two parts is predicted by the two legs, as explained above, but that does not explain why each half of the empire fell before its enemies (West, before Odoacer in 476; East, before the Turks in 1453, with the fall of Constantinople); nor does it explain the persistence of Rome in the interim without any definite seats of authority—i.e., clay mixed with iron is essential to the understanding of the fall of the "iron kingdom."

The verse before us (v. 41) says that "the kingdom shall be divided" because it is composed of iron and clay. It was because the iron of Roman imperium (militaristic force as seen today in totalitarian systems) was mixed with the brittle weakness of clay (the popular will, fickle and easily molded, as seen today in communistic appeals to the common man), that the West and then the East fell (because of lack of internal cohesion). And Rome has continued "divided" into many parts by these two diverse principles, but the important thing is that Rome has continued.

Rome has persisted in the unsatisfactory and weak condition of inward division, but she has persisted! As Urquhart expressed it: "The whole of Western Europe adopted the language of the Romans, and its inhabitants looked upon themselves as Romans. The laws and institutions of Rome acquired such a power and durability that even at the present moment they still continue to maintain their influence upon millions of men. Such a development is without parallel in the history of the world."

Rome persisted in the Holy Roman Empire, with all of its weakness, attesting the truth of verse 41, and especially has the Roman (Catholic) Church perpetuated the language, spirit, idolatries, and culture of Rome.

Charlemagne sought to regroup the southern European nations of the old Roman Empire in A.D. 800 in a union which later became known as the Holy Roman Empire. This persisted through medieval times until after the Reformation. A period of nationalistic emphasis, with antagonism heightened by colonial expansion jealousies, characterized the further history of Europe from that time into the modern period. Bitter national envy and hatred carried on into the twentieth century and had a real share in precipitating World Wars I and II. This was especially true of Germany and France (War of 1870, World Wars I and II).

Thus, the "feet" period of the fourth kingdom is the period between the disruption of old Rome and the revival of Rome in its final form.

THIRD PERIOD: "Toes (ten) . . . of iron mixed with potter's clay" (2:42-43)=
REVIVED FINAL FORM OF FOURTH EMPIRE

Despite the "divided" condition of the West, Scripture makes it plain that "the deadly wound" of the dismembered empire is going to be "healed" to the consternation of all peoples (REVELATION 13:3-4). It matters little what the new empire will be called. It may, as we have suggested, be called "The United States of Europe," or "The United States of the Western World," but the empire is to be reconstituted, for the image smitten by the Stone (Christ) is envisioned as being totally intact when it is smitten on the ten toes, its final form. In my judgment it will comprise the whole Western world, all that was Rome and all that has come out of Rome. This would include the Western Hemisphere, which almost totally came out of Western Europe, the sphere of the *old* Roman world. This ten-divisioned form, represented by ten toes and ten "horns" (REVELATION 13:1; 17:12-17), is ten kings or kingdoms who cooperate with the Roman "beast" (leader) for an agreed purpose and period of time ("one hour"). At no time in Rome's history has she been divided into ten parts. This final form has not yet arrived, but is undoubtedly on the way. It is the revivified Western Entente which makes a treaty with Israel permitting the restoration of temple worship for a period of seven years (DANIEL 9:27). This inevitably involves a reconstituted Israel with a leader in Jerusalem called "the false prophet," who will be an ally of the western ruler whose capital is Rome (compare REVELATION 13, 17).

Much of this has taken place in the lifetime of many living today. The decline of colonial powers, the sustaining of which led to constant wars among the western nations, has well-nigh reached its conclusion. One by one the western nations have lost their colonies and have had all they can do to survive. Weakened by two world wars and pressed into the beginnings of unity by the threat of Russia, things are taking place at an accelerated rate which seemed far off a few years ago.

One of the few results of World War I in prophetic fulfillment was the freeing of Palestine from the Turkish yoke, permitting the return of Israel to Palestine. Despite tremendous odds, the nation was formed in 1948 and has withstood all attempts to dislodge her. Thus, we have two parallel events: (1) the revival of Israel on her own soil as a sovereign nation able to make treaties, and (2) the trend toward western unity, which will eventuate in a treaty with Israel concerning the restoration of temple worship.

III. Recent Progress Toward Fulfillment of the Prophecy of Western Unity

The need for unity has become increasingly apparent to the Western world, and with World War II, the United States and Latin America became very much related to all that goes on in Europe. Toward the close of World War II came Benelux, a working agremeent between Belgium, the Netherlands, and Luxembourg. This was followed swiftly by Western European Union in 1948 and NATO in 1949. At this point the United States became a prime mover in the drive toward western unity. No less a person than the great General Eisenhower was the first chief of staff of the North Atlantic Treaty Organization.

Following this came the European Coal and Steel Community (1952), while in 1954 the European Defense Community was aborted, only because of the multiple political divisions of a weak, pre-de Gaulle France. Finally, steps were taken to form the six-member Common Market, which has recently reported itself from eighteen months to three years ahead of schedule in its fast pace toward economic unity. Signed on no less a place than Capitoline Hill, Rome's ancient government seat, originally by six nations, now expanded to ten, it has become a potent force in challenging Communist attempts to bankrupt the Western world through discount-house methods, playing nation against nation in harmful competition. Now ten nations of 180,000,000 people are working as a unit in European and world commerce and challenging Russia successfully.

Despite the intransigence of de Gaulle in his ill will against Britain and the United States, there can be no doubt that these two great nations will necessarily join the Common Market to cooperate for the common good. The fiscal future of the whole Western world depends upon such a union of efforts.

Thus, in a few brief years we have had *military* union in the form of NATO, with its common command, common weapons, and common uniform; we have had *economic* union in the form of the Common Market, which must shortly embrace England and America. There remains only the final step of *political* union. Few seem aware that immediately following World War II first steps were taken in planning a representative parliament of the Western world. Moving spirits in this drive were Paul Henri Spaak of Belgium, Jean Monnet of France, and Winston Churchill of England. The situation is much like that of our original colonies prior to the American Revolution. Cooperation is fine, but is too slow and has its hazards. The various sovereign states must come to the place where they see that the only solution to their problems is to delegate their powers to a federal union. When this takes place, the

final step of union—political union—will have taken place and the
Western world will fulfill the prophecy of the "deadly wound
healed."

This latter is as inevitable as the incoming tide. The Western
Hemisphere will be part of this revived fourth "empire." Not a
fundamentalist, prophetic teacher, but a keen secular observer of
international events (Chet Huntley) spoke the following words in
a broadcast on May 2, 1956—words which carry an even more
ringing sound to clear-thinking people today, quite apart from
prophetic teaching:

> By treaty, by past, by tradition, by promise, by sentiment, by
> civilization, heritage, language, custom, and purpose, we are
> today bound to Europe. A loose coalition of states will not
> do. The formation of an Atlantic Community is the logical
> conclusion. This reporter can recall most vividly the debate
> when the European Defense Community was almost a real-
> ity. I have only to recall the speeches of Monnet (of
> France), Henri Spaak (of Belgium), and De Gasperi (of
> Italy), through which ran the steady premise that a federated
> Europe could alone become a reality when it is joined by
> Britain and the United States in an Atlantic Community.

To the student of prophecy the shape of things to come is
becoming increasingly plain. Therefore, a United States of Europe, yea, of the Western world, must come. Typical of the complete change of climate is a little news item of a few years back
which went unobserved by most people. It told of West Germany
being invited by France to train her troops on *French* soil! Knowing the galling pain and hate of their three wars (Franco-Prussian
of 1870, and World Wars I and II), this is nothing short of a
miracle! As late as 1955 any such possibility would have been
scoffed at. But such things are now reality, and the world is moving swiftly toward the events prophesied by Daniel and other
prophets.

Just how far these things will proceed before the Lord returns
for His Church we cannot know. The cycle could swing the other
way. But, if it should, it will return again. At any event, the
Western world as revivified Rome (it matters not under what
name) will make a treaty with Israel for one seven-year period.

The final form of the revived empire will be a ten-divisioned form pictured by ten toes (DANIEL 2) and ten horns (DANIEL 7; REVELATION 13, 17). Some think the ten-divisioned form will not come till about the middle of the Seventieth Week. But in any event, in the middle of the week the Jewish leader will traitorously double-cross his people and break the treaty (DANIEL 9:27) by desecrating the sanctuary through setting up in the temple an image of the political leader of the Western Empire (the one with headquarters in Rome, MATTHEW 24:15; REVELATION 13). He will persecute with devilish cruelty all who refuse to worship the image (REVELATION 13; MATTHEW 24:16-22, esp. v. 21). This period is called the Great Tribulation, the Time of Jacob's Trouble.

This latter half of the week will be the occasion for the hellish, Satan-inspired form of empire, which will specialize in persecution of believers and blasphemy of heaven and its Christ. These ten kings (kingdoms) shall give their power to the beast "for one hour" (i.e., one agreed period) (REVELATION 17:12-14).

This final form of the empire will continue till Christ returns to earth as the Smiting Stone.

So, pilgrims, lift up your heads. Your redemption draweth nigh!

XIV

The Prophetic Word

Stephen F. Olford

For we have not followed cunningly devised fables, when we made known unto you the power and coming of our Lord Jesus Christ, but were eyewitnesses of his majesty.

For he received from God the Father honour and glory, when there came such a voice to him from the excellent glory, This is my beloved Son, in whom I am well pleased.

And this voice which came from heaven we heard, when we were with him in the holy mount.

We have also a more sure word of prophecy; whereunto ye do well that ye take heed, as unto a light that shineth in a dark place, until the day dawn, and the daystar arise in your hearts:

Knowing this first, that no prophecy of the Scripture is of any private interpretation.

For the prophecy came not in old time by the will of man: but holy men of God spake as they were moved by the Holy Ghost. (II PETER 1:16-21)

To arrive at any understanding of the doctrine of the Lord's return, it is necessary that we should examine what the Bible means by the Prophetic Word. Although other New Testament writers deal variously with this subject, it is Peter who best defines the term. And so I propose to draw your attention to the verses we have just read.

Let us remember that Peter wrote this epistle not only to encourage persecuted Christians in their spiritual life and to warn against false teachers and doctrines, but to emphasize the glorious hope of the Lord's return. In chapter 3 especially, we find the advent truth assailed (vv. 1-4), then the advent truth attested (vv.

5-10), and finally, the advent truth applied (v. 11-18). Here in this first chapter, however, he considers the certainty, character, and challenge of the Prophetic Word. Let us now examine these.

The Certainty of the Prophetic Word

"We have also a more sure word of prophecy . . ." (v. 19). With a ring of confidence, Peter vividly sets forth the twofold basis of the certainty of the Prophetic Word. To start with, there is *the reality of the first advent.* "For we have not followed cunningly devised fables, when we made known unto you the power and coming of our Lord Jesus Christ, but were eyewitnesses of his majesty" (v. 16; see also vv. 17-18).

To Peter, the fact that the Lord Jesus had come once was an evident proof that He would come again. He and two other disciples, James and John, had been eyewitnesses of the Saviour's honor and glory. They had heard heaven's commendation of Jesus Christ as God's beloved Son; but Peter here maintains that such seeing and hearing of the power and majesty of Christ were not to be compared with the ". . . more sure word of prophecy . . ." (v. 19). In other words, the reality of the first advent made even more certain the reality of the second advent.

The "word of prophecy" to which Peter refers is the body of the Old Testament teaching concerning the coming again of the Lord Jesus. Dr. A. T. Pierson points out that the prophecies and references to Christ in the Old Testament, which are expressly cited in the New Testament, either as predictions fulfilled in Christ or as previsions applied to Him, number no less than 333. Pierson goes on to say that if there are 333 prophetic statements concerning the first coming of Christ, then there are at least double that number which relate to His second coming. So Peter exclaims, "We have also a *more sure* word of prophecy . . ." (v. 19). The reality of the first coming of Christ was his ground for believing even more confidently in the second coming. Paul in his first letter to the Thessalonians employs a similar argument when he writes: "For if we believe that Jesus died and rose again, even so them also which sleep in Jesus will God bring with him. For this we say unto you by the word of the Lord, that we which are alive and remain unto the coming of the Lord shall not prevent them which are asleep. For the Lord himself shall descend from heaven with a shout . . ." (I THESSALONIANS 4:14-16).

Peter's confidence in the certainty of the Prophetic Word is based not only upon the reality of the first advent, but also on *the necessity of the second advent.* "We have also a more sure word of prophecy . . ." (v. 19). It is of singular significance that Peter uses the event of the transfiguration to support his contention that Jesus must return to this earth. No one knew better than Peter that the first coming of Christ was characterized by humiliation, sorrow, and death. And yet, on that one memorable occasion when Jesus was transfigured before His three favored disciples, Peter had witnessed something of the majesty, honor, and glory which were never seen throughout the earthly ministry of Christ. In view of this, Peter insisted in this second letter of his that the return of Christ is a sheer necessity. So he speaks of ". . . the power and coming of 'the' Lord Jesus Christ . . ." (v. 16).

In the very nature of things, the Christ of grace must be manifested as the Christ of glory; the Christ of humility must be demonstrated as the Christ of honor; the Christ of redeeming love must be vindicated as the Christ of reigning life. Or, in the language of Frances Ridley Havergal, we can imagine Peter saying:

> O the joy to see Thee reigning,
> Thee, my own beloved Lord!
> Every tongue Thy Name confessing,
> Worship, honor, glory, blessing
> Brought to Thee with glad accord;
> Thee, my Master and my Friend,
> Vindicated and enthroned;
> Unto earth's remotest end
> Glorified, adored, and owned.

Thus the certainty of the Prophetic Word is clearly based upon the reality of the first and the necessity for the second advent.

The Character of the Prophetic Word

". . . No prophecy of the Scripture is of any private interpretation. For the prophecy came not in old time by the will of man: but holy men of God spake as they were moved by the Holy Ghost" (vv. 20-21).

It is the tendency of many people to regard prophetic pronouncements, as well as predictions, with skepticism and incredulity. To some extent this attitude of mind has been justified by the fantastic misinterpretations and misapplications of prophetic teaching throughout the history of the church. On the other hand, to the simple Bible-lover who approaches this great truth with a humble spirit, an open mind, and an obedient heart, there need be no doubt or nebulous thinking; for Peter tells us here that the character of the Prophetic Word is divinely safeguarded.

In the first place, the Prophetic Word is *divinely inspired.* "For . . . prophecy came not in old time by the will of man: but holy men of God spake as they were moved by the Holy Ghost" (v. 21). The body of prophetic teaching throughout the Bible is not of man's devising; on the contrary, holy men were so caught up and controlled by the Holy Spirit that they wrote supernaturally and infallibly. At times they wrote above and beyond their own experience. Peter refers to this in his first epistle, when he states: ". . . the prophets have inquired and searched diligently, who prophesied of the grace that should come unto you: searching what, or what manner of time the Spirit of Christ which was in them did signify, when it testified beforehand the sufferings of Christ, and the glory that should follow" (I PETER 1:10-11). And then in the passage we are considering, he says: ". . . men spake from God, being moved by the Holy Ghost" (v. 21). The word "moved" is one of the picture words of the New Testament. It is precisely the same word which is translated in the Acts of the Apostles as "driven." You remember that in the graphic chapter which describes a shipwreck, there comes this very suggestive phrase: ". . . fearing lest they should fall into the quicksands, struck sail, and so *were driven*" (ACTS 27:17). That is the word which is here translated "moved." This does not suggest that holy men were robots or machines, since their personalities shine through their prophetic utterances, but it does mean that they spake from God, or "out of God." Their speech was born in God, God-driven and God-controlled, so that their word was sure, certain, and authoritative.

In the second instance, the Prophetic Word is *divinely interpreted.* ". . . No prophecy of the Scripture is of any private interpretation" (v. 20). This indicates that in order to understand the Prophetic Word, we need the aid of the Holy Spirit and the support of comparative Scriptures. Only the Holy Spirit can guide men into all truth. Jesus said, ". . . when he, the Spirit of Truth, is come, he will guide you into all truth: for he shall not speak of himself; but whatsoever he shall hear, that shall he speak: and he will show you things to come" (JOHN 16:13). And Paul tells us that to understand the words which the Holy Ghost teaches, we must compare spiritual things with spiritual (1 CORINTHIANS 2:13).

How vital it is, then, to approach not only prophetic teaching, but all teaching, with minds that are free from prejudice and preconceptions, relying only on the plain statements of Scripture and the personal guidance of the Holy Spirit.

The Challenge of the Prophetic Word

"We have also a more sure word of prophecy; whereunto ye do well that ye take heed, as unto a light that shineth in a dark place, until the day dawn, and the daystar arise in your hearts" (v. 19).

There is nothing more challenging in the whole Scripture than the Prophetic Word. So Peter exhorts that we are to take heed to it, for wherever we find this light, it is *a searching light,* ". . . a light that shineth in a dark place" (or more literally, a light that shineth in squalor, v. 19).

There is no truth more searching than that of the Lord's return. In personal life, this prophetic light exposes anything and everything that would make us ashamed at the coming of Christ. This is what John means when he tells his readers to ". . . abide in [Christ]; that, when he shall appear, [they] may have confidence, and not be ashamed before him at his coming" (1 JOHN 2:28). How can a Christian await the return of Christ with an unforgiving spirit, an immoral life, a disorderly walk, or an unsurrendered body, or an unfulfilled task? But this searching light exposes not only the sin and squalor in personal life, but also general life. The more we understand the truth of the coming again of the Lord Jesus, the more we shall become aware of the increasingly dark, sinful, and squalid world around us.

The unregenerate man wistfully hopes for Utopia or the age of prosperity, and seems to think that by a process of evolution such a golden era will be ushered in. But alas, the Scriptures give no such hope. On the contrary, the Word tells us that ". . . in the last days perilous times shall come . . . evil men and seducers shall wax worse and worse, deceiving, and being deceived" (II TIMOTHY 3:1, 13). The nominally religious person thinks that the world eventually is going to be converted, and so he works feverishly to bring this about. But the fact of the matter is that God has never promised the conversion of the world in this age. What the Bible does teach is that God has visited ". . . the Gentiles, to take out of them a people for his name" (ACTS 15:14). But while this activity of the Spirit is going on, let us remember that ". . . the mystery of iniquity doth already work . . ." (II THESSALONIANS 2:7). The spirit of the Antichrist is already operating in the world, and sin, squalor, and wickedness will therefore abound more and more.

To the genuine believer, all these signs are but a herald of the Saviour's coming. The Christian recognizes that the darkest hours always precede the dawn. Instead of getting better, the world is going to get worse. The church will experience revival (JAMES 5:7-8) and souls will be won from every part of the earth, but the light of prophecy will increasingly show up the hideous wickedness of a world that is fast moving to destruction. How this should challenge us to hold forth the Word of life and shine as lights in the dark world around us!

But this prophetic light is also *a saving light*, ". . . a light that shineth in a dark place, until the day dawn . . ." (v. 19). While this light searches and exposes the sin around, it also anticipates the coming dawn. Paul speaks of that "day dawn" as the day of salvation. To the believer, salvation comprehends the past, present, and future. In the past we are saved from the penalty of sin; in the present we are being saved from the power of sin; in the future we shall be saved from the presence of sin. Consider the Apostle's words: ". . . it is high time to awake out of sleep: for now is our salvation nearer than when we believed. The night is far spent, the day is at hand: let us therefore cast off the works of darkness, and let us put on the armor of light" (ROMANS 13:11-12).

Here is the saving light of prophecy. The "day dawn" is coming. The hour of our "redemption draweth nigh" (LUKE 21:28). In view of this we must *wake up*—". . . awake out of sleep . . ." (ROMANS 13:11); *get up*—for "the night is far spent, the day is at hand . . ." (ROMANS 13:12); *dress up*—". . . put on the armor of light" (ROMANS 13:12), which is holy living, and then *look up*—". . . lift up [our] heads; for [our] redemption draweth nigh" (LUKE 21:28).

One last thought is that this prophetic light is *a satisfying light,* ". . . a light that shineth in a dark place, until the day dawn, and the daystar arise in your hearts" (v. 19). Some commentators prefer to link the phrase "your hearts" with the injunction "take heed." This interpretation undoubtedly has merit. But I believe the other reading also has a truth for us. "The daystar" is none other than Jesus our Lord. At His first coming He called Himself "the dayspring from on high" (LUKE 1:78); at His second coming He is to be known as "the bright and morning star" (REVELATION 22:16). Christ, then, is "the daystar" of our hearts. And as the light of prophecy points to that rising star, our hearts leap within us, for the star has always been the symbol of that which satisfies the heart. So we can sing with David, ". . . I shall be satisfied, when I awake, with thy likeness" (PSALM 17:15). As John says, ". . . when he shall appear, we shall be like him; for we shall see him as he is" (1 JOHN 3:2). What a day that will be! And what a challenge now to prepare ourselves for the appearing of that "daystar." "Every man that hath this hope in him purifieth himself, even as he is pure" (1 JOHN 3:3).

Here, then, is the challenge of the Prophetic Word. With its certainty, character, and challenge, let us submit ourselves in coming days not only to its study, but also to its searching, saving, and satisfying light. Only thus shall we abide in Christ and not be ashamed at His coming.

XV

The Coming of Christ

Stephen F. Olford

Paul, and Silvanus, and Timotheus, unto the church of the Thessalonians which is in God the Father, and in the Lord Jesus Christ: Grace be unto you, and peace, from God our Father, and the Lord Jesus Christ.

We give thanks to God always for you all, making mention of you in our prayers; remembering without ceasing your work of faith, and labor of love, and patience of hope in our Lord Jesus Christ, in the sight of God and our Father; knowing, brethren, beloved, your election of God.

For our gospel came not unto you in word only, but also in power, and in the Holy Ghost, and in much assurance; as ye know what manner of men we were among you for your sake.

And ye became followers of us, and of the Lord, having received the word in much affliction, with joy of the Holy Ghost: so that ye were ensamples to all that believe in Macedonia and Achaia.

For from you sounded out the word of the Lord not only in Macedonia and Achaia, but also in every place your faith to God-ward is spread abroad; so that we need not to speak any thing.

For they themselves show of us what manner of entering in we had unto you, and how ye turned to God from idols to serve the living and true God; and to wait for his Son from heaven, whom he raised from the dead, even Jesus, which delivered us from the wrath to come. (1 THESSALONIANS 1:1-10)

This Epistle was penned by the Apostle Paul from Corinth shortly after he had concluded a crusade for Christ in the city of Thessalonica (A.D. 54). It is not only the earliest of his letters, but the

finest illustration of his depth and richness of teaching in primitive
evangelism to be found anywhere in the New Testament.

When we consider that Paul had been in Thessalonica for not
more than three weeks (ACTS 17:1-9) among antagonistic Jews
and idolatrous pagans, we cannot but be impressed with the areas
of truth that he must have covered, by reason of the fact that he
refers again and again to the great doctrines that he had imparted
to them. Prominent among these tenets of the faith was the second
coming of Christ. Indeed, our text implies that his converts accepted from the very beginning that this was part of the saving
gospel of Christ. Reminding them of the miracle of conversion
which had taken place, Paul says: ". . . ye turned to God from
idols to serve the living and true God; and to wait for his Son from
heaven . . ." (vv. 9, 10). Now what did Paul mean by the words,
"wait for his Son from heaven" (v. 10)? To answer this question,
let us look first at:

The Subjects of This Waiting

"Wait for his Son from heaven . . ." (v. 10). The immediate
context gives us the answer to this first question. The only people
who qualify to wait for the return of Christ are men and women
who have experienced *the repudiation of the old life.* "*Ye turned
from idols* to serve the living and true God" (v. 9). An idol has
been defined as anything which takes the place of the living and
true God. The city of Thessalonica was full of them, and every
one represented some form of lust, vice, or sin; so that in the last
analysis these idols were the attempt of men and women to satisfy
their hunger for God in their own perverted ways.

Where is your idol? Is it a good bank account? Is it the fulfillment of sexual desires? Is it worldly pleasure? Is it social status?
Is it just the worship of self?

When Paul preached the transforming gospel of Christ in Thessalonica, we read that his hearers ". . . turned to God from idols
. . ." (v. 9). There was a repudiation of the old life. Nothing less
than this is genuine conversion. We have no right to recognize the
Christian testimony of anyone who cannot witness to a definite
renunciation of the old life.

Such people must also have experienced *the reception of the new life.* "Ye turned to God from idols to serve *the living and true God*" (v. 9). The word "serve" denotes the complete subjection of the will to the sovereignty of Another. It is the beginning of a new life. Once slaves to false and dead gods, these Thessalonians were now utterly committed to the true and living God. Paul goes right on to say that such a transforming experience had come about only through the risen Christ who had delivered and continues to deliver "from the wrath to come" (v. 10). The present tense in the original emphasizes the glorious truth of an ever-present and powerful Saviour from sin, death, and judgment.

Tell me, have you experienced this reception of the new life in Christ the Deliverer? Have you been saved? Are you being saved? Have you the assurance that you will yet be saved? Unless you can answer with an unqualified "yes," then you are not entitled "to wait for God's Son from heaven." In fact, nothing could be more terrible than the return of Jesus Christ. For you, that would mean final condemnation and damnation. What you need is conversion: a repudiation of the old life and a reception of a new life in Christ.

A young girl desiring baptism and membership in a church in Scotland was being interviewed by the board of elders. Because she was so young, they wanted to be quite sure that she knew what she was doing, so they asked: "Did you ever find out that you were a sinner?" "Yes," she replied without hesitation, "I did indeed!" "Well," the brethren continued, "have you experienced a change?" "Yes, I have," was the immediate answer. "Then there is another question that we wish to put to you," said the men: "are you still a sinner?" to which she answered, "Yes, I am a saved sinner." "How would you describe the change?" pressed the elders. "Well, it's like this," confessed the girl, "before I was saved I was running after sin. Now I am running away from it!" This is true conversion, for it involves a change of both attitude and direction.

So we have seen what we mean by the subjects of this waiting. But now consider, further:

The Objects of This Waiting

"Wait for his Son from heaven . . ." (v. 10). Have you ever wondered why it is that God does not take His people home as soon as they are saved? The answer to that question is that He waits to test and prove our love to Christ, while we are still in the world and in the flesh and in daily conflict with the devil.

Writing his last letter to Timothy, Paul dramatically contrasts the love of the appearing of Christ with the love of the world in which we live. Speaking of his departure, Paul says: "For I am now ready to be offered, and the time of my departure is at hand. I have fought a good fight, I have finished my course, I have kept the faith: henceforth there is laid up for me a crown of righteousness, which the Lord, the righteous judge, shall give me at that day: and not to me only, but unto all them also that love his appearing" (II TIMOTHY 4:6-8. And then with heavy heart he adds, "Demas hath forsaken me, having loved this present world . . ." (v. 10).

Now God, who is omniscient, knows that some people need longer than others to prove their love; so the duration of life varies. But for all the test is "loving His appearing." It is one thing to say that we love Jesus, but it is quite another to love His appearing. We can say we love our Lord, but can we say with equal confidence that we are eagerly awaiting the day when we can look into His face and hear His "Well done"?

If you were to question my son as to whether or not he loved his father, I know that he would answer in the affirmative without a moment's hesitation. But I question seriously whether he could equally love my appearing, if I happened to come and find him doing something which he knew to be displeasing to me.

Among the many ways revealed in the New Testament in which we can demonstrate our love to Christ while we "wait," there are three of comprehensive significance.

We must serve the purpose of Christ on earth. And Jesus said, ". . . Occupy till I come" (LUKE 19:13). These words occur in the parable of the ten pounds, and were employed by our Lord to press home His call to Christian stewardship during His absence from His waiting church. The Greek word means "do business," and suggests devotion to the call of Christ to serve His purpose while here on earth. The Master expects us to invest everything we have in His business, so that we shall not be ashamed before Him at His coming. This purpose for our lives concerns both our character and our service. If we truly love His appearing, we will occupy till He comes.

We must share the passion of Christ on earth. "For as often as ye eat this bread, and drink this cup, ye do *show the Lord's death till he come*" (1 CORINTHIANS 11:26, italics added). The object for which the Saviour instituted this feast of remembrance was to keep His people ever at the foot of the Cross and identified with His redemptive passion. No one can take the broken bread and the outpoured wine without exclaiming with the Apostle Paul: Oh, "that I might know him, and the power of his resurrection, and the *fellowship of his sufferings*, being made conformable unto his death" (PHILIPPIANS 3:10, italics added).

There is a suffering for our sin, which is punishment. There is another suffering for our Lord, which is persecution; but in the third place, there is a suffering *with* Christ, which is passion. This identification with Jesus in His redemptive concern for a lost world is the highest privilege that a Christian can enjoy. So as we celebrate the Holy Communion we are to be reminded of our call to share the Lord's passion till He come.

We must show the power of Christ on earth. "But that which ye have already, *hold fast till I come*" (REVELATION 2:25, italics added). To understand this exhortation, we must examine the context. The members of the church at Thyatira in Asia Minor were in difficulties. Their loyalty to the church of Christ was being threatened by the conflicting interests and pressures of their contemporary world. Thyatira was an industrial city renowned for its many trade guilds, and to be in any kind of business at all involved belonging to one of these guilds. But the problem for the Christian was that any association with these trade unions inevitably meant eating meals dedicated to pagan deities and participating in unspeakable licentiousness and debauchery, in which these banquets culminated. Now, every believer knew that the church of Christ was a company of separated people who could not compromise with the world. So the risen Lord appeared to His church and said, ". . . hold fast till I come" (REVELATION 2:25). In other

words, "If ye love Me, show My power on earth by being steadfast
and keeping the church pure."

So we see that the supreme objects of "waiting for God's Son
from heaven" are to serve the Lord's purpose till He comes, share
the Lord's passion till He comes, and show the Lord's power till
He comes. This, in practical terms, is loving His appearing; this is
"waiting for God's Son from heaven."

Our last thought concerns:

The Prospects of This Waiting

"Wait for his Son from heaven . . ." (v. 10). We may well ask,
"How long are we to wait? Has the Bible any light on this matter?" The answer, of course, is that it has, for all who have eyes to
see! To sum up this teaching as comprehensively and concisely as
possible, let us put it in this form: Christians are to wait for the
coming of the Lord until *the recruitment of all the saints*. "Simeon
hath declared how God at the first did visit the Gentiles, to take
out of them a people for his name. And to this agree the words of
the prophets; as it is written, After this I will return, and will build
again the tabernacle of David, which is fallen down; and I will
build again the ruins thereof, and I will set it up" (ACTS 15:14-
16). This is one of the most important and significant passages in
the New Testament regarding the church and the coming of
Christ. The words were spoken by James at the first church council in Jerusalem. He was describing to the gathered delegates what
God had revealed to Peter concerning the divine purpose for the
opening and closing of this church age. It all began at Pentecost
when the church was founded. Ever since then, the Spirit of God
has been calling out men and women from every nation under
heaven throughout succeeding generations. But the statement also
tells us how the church is going to be consummated. "After this I
will return. . . ." When the last believer is added to the body of
Christ, Jesus will come again. That "last one" may be added
today. Are you working and waiting for this?

A minister once entered an ancient almshouse of which an aged
couple were the inmates. Beside a little round table opposite the fire
sat the husband, too paralyzed to move. His wooden shoe pattered

on the floor, keeping time with his trembling frame. As he was very deaf the visitor shouted in his ear, "Well, my friend, what are you doing?" With a radiant smile the old man looked up and said, "Waiting, sir!" "For what?" asked the minister. The answer was speedy and fervent, "For the appearing of my Lord." Here was the dear old saint not anticipating death but waiting for God's Son from heaven. So Christians are to wait until the recruitment of all the saints.

But in the second place they are to wait *the fulfillment of all the signs*. "And when these things begin to come to pass, then look up, and lift up your heads; for your redemption draweth nigh" (LUKE 21:28). These words were spoken by our Lord in what is known as the Olivet Discourse. The events depicted are to be the prelude to the great tribulation which is going to be visited upon the Jews ere they are delivered and restored to their Messiah. But long before this the church will have been raptured by the coming again of Jesus *for* His saints.

Now while ". . . it is not for [us] to know the times or the seasons, which the Father hath put in his own power" (ACTS 1:7), *there are signs* which are to herald the coming of Christ. They are many and varied and often repeated throughout succeeding generations. Some, however, are especially related to the final days before the Lord descends with a shout and with the voice of the archangel and with the trump of God. Think of *the increase of travel and speed*. "But thou, O Daniel, shut up the words, and seal the book, even to the time of the end: many shall run to and fro, and knowledge shall be increased" (DANIEL 12:4). "The chariots shall rage in the streets, they shall justle one against another in the broad ways: they shall seem like torches, they shall run like the lightnings"(NAHUM 2:4). Never in human history have we seen such phenomenal advances in travel and speed as in our generation. Very soon, so we are informed, we shall be attempting the moon shot, and God alone knows what after that. This is a sign of the last days.

The spread of literacy and knowledge. As we have seen from Daniel, "knowledge shall be increased" (12:4), and then Paul adds in his Epistle to Timothy that there will be people "ever learning, and never able to come to the knowledge of the truth" (II TIMOTHY 3:7). There are more people reading today than ever before. And then what shall we say of the transmission of knowledge through radio, television, tapes, and research? In spite of all this learning and knowledge, however, there is increasing resistance to the liberating gospel—another sign of the last days.

The unprecedented wars and rumors of wars. "Then . . . nation shall rise against nation, and kingdom against kingdom" (LUKE 21:10) There has rarely been a time when a war was not being fought somewhere, but only in our day has war been global, and the next will be so utterly destructive and unthinkably extensive that many believe that God will have to precipitate such an event with the descent of His own Son. If this be true, then the nearer we come to the next war, the closer we approach to the coming again of Jesus Christ.

The restoration of the Jews to Palestine. "Therefore, behold, the days come, saith the Lord . . . I will bring [my people] again into their land that I gave unto their fathers" (JEREMIAH 16:14-16; LUKE 21:29-31). The return of the Jews to their own land has never been possible until recently. And the happenings that have taken place in that country since the Israeli state was constituted and recognized are among the most significant signs of our time. Vast preparations are under way to prepare for the coming of the Messiah. Even though blind to the fact that Jesus has already come as Saviour, Orthodox Jews are awaiting what will prove to be His second coming. And we are told that ". . . they shall look on him whom they pierced, and they shall mourn for him . . ." ZECHARIAH 12:10). Here, then, is a very significant sign of the times.

Many other signs could be cited, but these will suffice to show us how the future is shaping. The question is, when will the last sign be fulfilled?

To illustrate the relevance of these happenings to the near return of our Lord, Harold Wildish tells a lovely story of a father who had to leave his home and go on a long journey. Just before he left, his little three-year-old son asked him, "Daddy, when will you be coming back?" Now, the father knew that he would not be back until the end of September. However, he realized it would be of little use to talk about times and seasons to his little boy, for he would not know the difference between them. The father said to the boy, "Now listen; when you see the leaves on the trees turning red and brown and beginning to fall to the ground, then you can be sure that Daddy is coming back very soon."

The next day the father left home. During the months of July and August the little boy would go for walks with his nurse. On these walks he used to talk about his absent Daddy. Slowly the weeks went by until it came early September, and then mid-September. Although the boy did not notice it, the leaves on the trees were changing colors.

Then one night there was a big windstorm and millions of leaves came down, filling the sidewalks and gutters. The next morning when the little fellow went out, he immediately saw them. Letting go his nurse's hand, he went among the leaves and began to kick them sky high. Then he began to shout, "Hurrah! Hurrah! Daddy is coming soon!"

Likewise, all over the world there is an expectation. The leaves are turning brown and they are beginning to fall. Jesus said, ". . . when ye see these things," be gloomy? No, chins up! "Lift up your heads." The great future of every child of God may be dawning, "for the coming of the Lord draweth near."

So we have considered what we mean by waiting for God's Son from heaven. In the light of such challenging and searching truth, I want to ask you: are you ready for His coming? If not, will you pray this simple prayer:

> Coming suddenly, coming soon;
> Coming certainly, night or noon.
> Jesus, I humbly pray,
> Take all my sins away
> And keep me till that day
> When Thou shalt come.

XVI

The Resurrection and Translation of the Church

John F. Walvoord

The prophetic hope of those who trust in Christ in the present age is one of the great themes of prophecy. Many prophetic Scriptures, of course, refer to the course of the Gentiles as revealed in the prophecies of Daniel. Many other prophecies relate to the program of God for Israel, beginning with the promise to Abraham of the promised land and culminating in the millennial kingdom. Distinct from the great prophecies relating to the Gentiles and to Israel is the line of truth relating to the church as the body of Christ.

The doctrine of the second coming of Christ to the earth is taught in both Testaments and is implied in all of the hundreds of verses dealing with the future millennial kingdom on earth. The New Testament, however, introduces for the first time the doctrine of the rapture, the revelation concerning the resurrection and translation of the saints of the present age. This constitutes the peculiar hope of saints living today that Christ may come at any moment to take them to Himself, with all that this portends for a glorious future in His Presence.

First Revelation of the Rapture

Although Christ introduced the subject of the second coming on numerous occasions in His public ministry and especially dealt with it in the Olivet Discourse in Matthew 24-25, the first mention of the rapture of the church is found in the last discourse of Christ before His death recorded in John 13–17. Here in John 14:2-3, Christ spoke the memorable words, "In my Father's house are many mansions: if it were not so, I would have told you. I go to prepare a place for you. And if I go and prepare a place for you, I will come again, and receive you unto myself; that where I am, there ye may be also." The disciples, troubled by the fact that Christ was going to leave them and they were not able to follow Him immediately (JOHN 13:36-38), had the wonderful hope that Christ would come to take them to Himself.

In this passage Christ announces that His purpose in leaving them is to go to the Father's house, here a reference to heaven or the immediate presence of God the Father. In heaven He would prepare a mansion (literally, an abiding place) for them. Just as surely as He was going to go to heaven, so He would come back to receive them unto Himself. As far as this revelation was concerned, they were to live in daily expectation of this wonderful future event. The testimony of the rest of the New Testament as well as the early Fathers illustrates how the early church took this promise literally, and looked for the coming of the Lord momentarily.

Although this introductory word did not contain any details, it is obvious even from this passage that the rapture of the church is quite different from the doctrine of the second coming of Christ to the earth. In His second coming to the earth, Christ would remain in the earthly scene to reign for a thousand years (REVELATION 20). By contrast, in the rapture He was to receive the disciples to Himself and take them to their heavenly home. The direction of the movement in the rapture is from earth to heaven, whereas in the second coming to the earth the saints come with Christ from heaven to the earth (REVELATION 19:11-21). It is quite obvious that the disciples did not completely understand this new pronouncement, as it was contrary to their previous expectation that Christ would remain on the earth and bring in His earthly Kingdom immediately. They did not understand at this time the difference between His first and second coming, although this had been embodied clearly in the previous teachings of Christ. Now their particular hope, however, was introduced, and their immediate expectation was not the millennial kingdom, but the return of Christ to take them to heaven.

Although the rapture of the church is mentioned frequently in the New Testament, for instance in every chapter of I and II Thessalonians, the major truths relating to this doctrine are found in two important passages, I Thessalonians 4:13-18 and I Corinthians 15:51-58.

The Resurrection of the Dead in Christ

In the Thessalonian passage the particular subject of the resurrection of Christians who die is discussed. It is apparent from this treatment that the Apostle Paul, in the few weeks he had been with the young Thessalonian church, had already introduced them to the wonderful hope that Christ was coming for them. What had not been comprehended, however, was how this event would relate to any of their number who died. They had been so occupied with the thought that Christ would come for the living that this apparently had not occurred to them. Since Paul had left Thessalonica, however, some of their number had died, possibly martyrs' deaths. Concerning these they now wanted instruction, and Timothy, who had been sent by Paul to inquire concerning their welfare, came back with this question to the Apostle. In reply the Apostle declared, "But I would not have you to be ignorant, brethren, concerning them which are asleep, that ye sorrow not, even as others which have no hope. For if we believe that Jesus died and rose again, even so them also which sleep in Jesus will God bring with him" (I THESSALONIANS 4:13-14). In contrast to contemporary indifference to eschatology, it is clear that God does want His own to know prophetic truth. Paul states he did not want the Thessalonians to be ignorant concerning their loved ones who had died in Christ. Their death is described as being "asleep," which by its very terminology implies the day of awakening or resurrection. He also links this with their immediate joy and comfort in that he does not want them to sorrow as others who have no hope. Here again is the sharp reminder that those outside of Christ have "no hope," in contrast to the wonderful hope that belongs to the Christian.

The certainty of the truth he is presenting is linked with the central doctrines of the death and resurrection in I Thessalonians 4:14. Although Christians may differ on minor points, it is obvious that there are certain great fundamentals of the faith. Among these are the fact that Jesus Christ died for our sins and rose again bodily from the grave. The Apostle Paul links the hope that we have in the coming of Christ to the certainty of these historic facts. Just as surely as Christ died and rose from the dead, so surely Christ will come again for His own. When He comes, according to I Thessalonians 4:14, God will bring with Christ those who "sleep in Jesus." By this expression he refers to physical death, but literally translated it is, "Sleep through Jesus." The implication is that they may have died because of their Christian faith and, therefore, may have been martyrs. The reference also might indicate the fact that their death is characterized as "sleep" because they are "in Jesus." Here is taught the wonderful truth that when Christ comes from heaven to the earth to receive living saints, as well as those who are raised from the dead, He will bring with him the souls and spirits of those who have died and have gone to heaven. In the passage that follows he deals with the subject of the resurrection, the reuniting of the immaterial part of man which has been in heaven with the material body which was laid in the grave.

One of the questions which the Thessalonian church had raised was the order of events. They apparently did not question the fact that their loved ones would be raised from the dead, nor did they question the fact that Christ was coming again. What they wanted to know was the order of these events. While it may be presuming too much upon this text to draw a certain conclusion, the assumption seems to be that the Thessalonians understood that there would be a time period in which there would be great trial and trouble in the earth prior to the second coming of Christ. They apparently also understood that the rapture would be before this event, though later they were disturbed by false teaching on this subject, as mentioned in II Thessalonians 2:1-3. What they did not know, however, was where in the order of these events (namely, the translation of the living, the tribulation which would follow, and the second coming of Christ to the earth) the resurrection of the loved ones in Christ would take place. In the Thessalonian passage Paul makes plain that they will not have to wait until after the tribulation for the resurrection of the dead in Christ. Instead, as the passage that follows indicates, the resurrection of the dead in Christ will occur just a moment before living Christians are translated.

This great revelation was a matter of special communication to Paul, for he writes in I Thessalonians 4:15, "For this we say unto you by the word of the Lord, that we which are alive and remain unto the coming of the Lord shall not prevent [precede] them which are asleep."

In the next passage he declares the order of events: "For the Lord himself shall descend from heaven with a shout, with the voice of the archangel, and with the trump of God: and the dead in Christ shall rise first: Then we which are alive and remain shall be caught up together with them in the clouds, to meet the Lord in the air: and so shall we ever be with the Lord" (1 THESSALONIANS 4:16-17).

According to this declaration, the rapture will begin with the Lord coming personally from heaven to the atmospheric heavens above the earth. He will issue a shout, literally a shout of command, which apparently is an order relating to the resurrection of the dead as well as the translation of the living. In the 11th chapter of John, in connection with the resurrection of Lazarus, it is recorded that Christ said, "Lazarus, come forth" (v. 43). As a result of this command, Lazarus was restored to life in the presence of the astounded witnesses. Earlier Christ had also predicted in John 5:25, "The hour is coming, and now is, when the dead shall hear the voice of the Son of God: and they that hear shall live." This refers to resurrection spiritually that occurs at the time of new birth. Going on from this, however, Christ added in John 5:28-29, "Marvel not at this: for the hour is coming, in which all that are in the grave shall hear his voice, and shall go forth; they that have done good, unto the resurrection of life; and they that have done evil, unto the resurrection of damnation." Someone has commented that if, at the resurrection of Lazarus, Christ had left off the name of Lazarus in His command, all of the dead would have come forth. The resurrection in I Thessalonians is also a selective resurrection, namely, the dead in Christ referred to in Philippians 3:11 where the resurrection of the dead, or the resurrection out from among the dead, is mentioned. It is clear at this time that the wicked dead are not raised, and there is a possibility, based on Daniel 12:1-2, that the Old Testament saints and tribulation saints will be raised after the tribulation rather than at this event. Although scholars differ on this point, it is clear that on this occasion all of those who have died in the present age are resurrected in obedience to the shout of command.

The event of the resurrection is accompanied, however, by "the voice of the archangel" and "the trump of God." No explanation is given of these events. It would be only natural, however, for the archangel, namely, Michael (JUDE 9), to give a shout of triumph on this great victory for the grace of God. In spite of all that Satan could do and in spite of the weakness of the flesh, here was the church triumphant, complete, and perfect in Christ. The voice of the archangel may be interpreted as the shout of victory.

The trump of God also mentioned may be the actual starting signal for the procession to move heavenward, in keeping with the military traditions of the Roman army as well as many parallels in the history of Israel.

The threefold event of the shout of the Lord, the voice of the archangel, and the trump of God combine to signal this great event. Paul states plainly that "the dead in Christ shall rise first," that is, they shall rise before the living saints are translated. Then, immediately following, perhaps seconds later, Paul declares, "Then we which are alive and remain shall be caught up together with them in the clouds, to meet the Lord in the air." Living saints as well as the dead in Christ are thus joined in one triumphant company as they meet the Lord in the air, and according to John 14 go to the Father's house to the place that is prepared for them.

Two great words of assurance climax this passage. First, the promise "so shall we ever be with the Lord." Separations are now over, both from loved ones in Christ and from the Lord Himself. No longer will we need to love One whom we have not seen, but Christians in that day will see the Lord in all His loveliness and glory. Second, on the basis of this future prospect Paul exhorts the grieving Thessalonians, "Wherefore comfort one another with these words" (I THESSALONIANS 4:18). The great hope of the Lord's return was to be a comfort to them in their separation from their loved ones, in that Christ may come any day. At the same time Paul gives them assurance of the glory and blessing that await those who have preceded them through death into the presence of the Lord.

The answer to the Thessalonians' question as to when the dead in Christ shall be raised is that they will be raised a moment before the living saints are translated. This is the glorious prospect of the church living and dead as it faces the critical hour in which we now live.

The Translation of the Living Church

The second major passage on the subject of the rapture and translation of the church is found in I Corinthians 15:15-58. This chapter, beginning with a restatement of the gospel of the death and resurrection of Christ (I CORINTHIANS 15:1-4) and continuing with a discussion of the resurrection of Christ, which occupies most of the chapter, forms a great theological background for the truth of the rapture. The main point that Paul is making is that it is normal for a death to be followed by resurrection, and that this is the plan and program of God. He argues that our present body is a natural body. It is a body given to dishonor and to corruption and to weakness. It needs to be transformed into a body of incorruption, of glory, of power, and of spirituality. Hence, death is followed by resurrection, and those thus raised receive a new body far better than the one that was laid in the tomb. The basic principle is laid down in I Corinthians 15:50, "Now this I say, brethren, that flesh and blood cannot inherit the kingdom of God; neither doth corruption inherit incorruption."

Following the discussion of resurrection, he takes up the important subject of the translation of the living. Although this was mentioned in I Thessalonians 4, here we have a more detailed description. The event of the rapture is described in I Corinthians 15:51-53 in these words, "Behold, I shew you a mystery; We shall not all sleep, but we shall all be changed, in a moment, in the twinkling of an eye, at the last trump: for the trumpet shall sound, and the dead shall be raised incorruptible, and we shall be changed. For this corruptible must put on incorruption, and this mortal must put on immortality."

Paul states that the truth he is presenting is "a mystery," that is, a truth not revealed in the Old Testament, but revealed in the New (cp. COLOSSIANS 1:26). The second coming of Christ to the earth to establish His kingdom on earth is no mystery, as this is plainly revealed in the Old Testament as well as in the New. The truth, however, of a special coming of Christ for those who are in this present age, an event preceding the tribulation, is a mystery, that is, a truth not hitherto revealed. Here is the explanation and detail of the preliminary promise given in John 14:2-3.

As Paul expounds the doctrine, he points out that all Christians shall not sleep, that is, die, but all Christians must be changed, in keeping with the doctrine previously laid down that our present bodies are not suited for heaven. The transforming event, where our bodies which are unsuited for heaven are translated into bodies fit for the presence of God, is described in the next few words. He declares the transformation will take place "in a moment, in the twinkling of an eye, at the last trump." The transformation will occur in a split second. At the occasion of Christ coming for His own, Christians will suddenly find that their bodies have been completely transformed. This is linked to the last trump, which may be identified with the trump mentioned in I Thessalonians 4:16. The marvelous result will be bodies that are immediately changed into the heavenly pattern.

In this and in other passages of Scripture it is clear that three major problems face a Christian in relation to his body prior to the translation. The bodies we have, of course, are sinful bodies. Paul refers to this in commenting on "The law of sin which is in my members" (ROMANS 7:23) and "the body of this death" (ROMANS 7:24). The body is subject to "the lusts of our flesh" (EPHESIANS 2:3). Such a body would not be suited for the holy presence of God.

Second, our present bodies are corruptible, that is, subject to decay and age. The normal course of life involves the deterioration of the human body from the time of birth and ultimately results in death. A corruptible body subject to decay and change is not suited for the eternal presence of God. Third, our bodies are mortal, that is, subject to physical death which can come accidentally or from a thousand natural causes. Such a body is not properly suited for eternity.

In the translation all three of these aspects are cared for immediately. Our bodies are made holy, incorruptible, and immortal. The purpose is stated in Ephesians 5:27, "That he might present it to himself a glorious church, not having spot, or wrinkle, or any such thing; but that it should be holy and without blemish." Our new bodies will be glorious, without spot or defilement, without wrinkle or sign of age, without blemish or natural disfiguration, without sin and holy.

The glorious victory of saints in Christ over death at the time of the rapture of the church is the subject of Paul's exultation in I Corinthians 14:54-57. When the rapture occurs, it will be a fulfillment at least in part of Isaiah 25:8, summarized in the statement, "death is swallowed up in victory." The Isaiah passage, of course, deals with the total victory which will not be brought about until all the saints have been raised at the conclusion of the millennium. The rapture of the church, however, is the first major victory in a series of tremendous triumphs over sin and death. Paul points out that while death is a result of sin, and sin in turn is related to the righteous law of God, in Christ there is victory over both, and sin and death will both be vanquished for those who put their trust in Christ.

Serving While Waiting

This important passage concludes with another exhortation, "Therefore, my beloved brethren, be ye stedfast, unmoveable, always abounding in the work of the Lord, forasmuch as ye know that your labour is not in vain in the Lord" (1 CORINTHIANS 15:58). In view of the wonderful hope that the Christian has of Christ coming for His own, and the transformation that will take place at that time with all the attendant circumstances, believers in Christ are exhorted to be steadfast, meaning "to be seated" or "to put full weight upon." This glorious truth will support all who put their trust in it. As a Christian faces the storms of life resting in these wonderful promises, he can be "unmoveable," resting in the ultimate victory which will be his in Christ. The rest of faith, however, does not mean inactivity or immobility, but it should rather spur us on to serve the Lord while we have time and opportunity. Hence, the believer in the rapture of the church should be "always abounding in the work of the Lord." This is a superlative statement, referring to ceaseless activity in the word "always" and in extent of labors "abounding." The truth of the rapture itself should remind Christians that ultimately they must give account of themselves to God, and their labor for Him will not be empty or vain. Those who are true students of prophecy will not be content simply with satisfying their curiosity or in finding comfort in their sorrow, but instead will be spurred on in their labors by the imminency of Christ's return and the obvious urgency of the task that remains.

As we are living in a day where so many evidences seem to point to the setting of the stage for the great world events which will follow the rapture of the church, surely the rapture itself may be very near. These words spoken so long ago are as up-to-date and contemporary as any portion of the Word of God. In a world that has many ominous portents of catastrophic events ahead, the Christian can look beyond the earth's horizon in the glory that awaits him in the presence of the Lord. Written plainly both in the Scriptures and in world events is the great truth, "It may be today."

XVII

The Church in Heaven

John F. Walvoord

The resurrection and translation of the church is only the beginning of tremendous events that greet the Christian as he contemplates the Prophetic Word. After the translation and resurrection of the saints and the new bodies that they will receive, and the unforgettable experience of seeing their Saviour face to face for the first time, their future experience will embody three basic truths: (1) Christians will begin a new relationship; (2) Christians will have new privileges; (3) Christians will have a new dwelling place.

The New Relationship: The Bridegroom and the Bride

In attempting to describe the wonderful relationship believers will have to their Lord and Saviour in heaven, the Scriptures use the symbolism of the church as a bride in relationship to Christ as the bridegroom. This is one of the seven major figures in Scripture relating Christ to the church, namely, the shepherd and the sheep, the vine and the branches, the cornerstone and the stones of the building, the high priest and the kingdom of priests, the head and the body, the last Adam and the new creation, and the bridegroom and the bride. Only the last named figure is basically eschatological, although it also has a contemporary significance.

In the Old Testament the symbol of marriage was used to describe the relationship of Israel to Jehovah; Israel in the Book of Hosea, for instance, is portrayed as the unfaithful wife of the Lord who will be restored in the future millennial kingdom.

In the New Testament the figure of marriage is used to relate Christ to the church, and believers in Christ are referred to as a virgin awaiting the future marriage to the bridegroom (II CORIN-

THIANS 11:2). The figure follows the oriental pattern of a marriage, in which there were three steps. The first or legal phase was that accomplished by the parents of the bride and the bridegroom when the dowry was paid and the parents of both parties agreed to the marriage. This step was the legal marriage and constituted the couple as man and wife even though they might not have seen each other. The procedure is illustrated in Abraham's securing a wife for Isaac, commissioning his servant to act for him. The present state of the church is that of a betrothed maiden awaiting the future coming of the bridegroom.

The second step in an oriental wedding occurred when the bridegroom, accompanied by his friends, proceeded in a processional to the home of the bride to take her from her home to his home. This is illustrated in Matthew 25 in the story of the ten virgins. The procession often would take place late at night and would consist in the bridegroom's claiming his bride. The third phase of an oriental wedding was the wedding feast, as in John 2 in the wedding at Cana. This often would take days, and was held on behalf of the visiting friends.

These three phases of the wedding correspond to the present position and prophetic hope of the church. At the present time the church is being prepared as a bride for her husband. The present process of progressive sanctification is described in Ephesians 5:26. The preceding verse declares that Christ "loved the church, and gave himself for it." The dowry payment, in the case of the church, was His precious blood shed on Calvary. This is followed by the present work of sanctification. In this life the church is sanctified and cleansed by the washing of water by the Word, that is, the application of the Scriptures to the spiritual experience of the church. The salvation and sanctification of the church are the preparation of the bride.

The second phase of the wedding will occur at the rapture, when Christ comes for His own, as in John 14:2-3 and I Thessalonians 4:17. In this great event Christ comes from heaven to the earth to claim His bride and take her to the Father's house. The third phase, the wedding feast, is mentioned in Revelation 19:7-9. This is actually not a wedding ceremony as often practiced in contemporary western civilization, but is the wedding feast, the third phase. Some regard this as taking place in heaven after the rapture, others picture it as fulfilled in the millennial reign of Christ. In either interpretation, it follows the rapture.

The implication of the symbolism corresponds to the view that the rapture occurs first, then the tribulation, and then the second coming of Christ to the earth. It is most significant that in connection with the announcement of the second coming of Christ to the earth it is the wedding feast that is announced—namely, the third aspect of the marriage, not the coming of Christ for His bride, which has previously taken place at the rapture. If the symbolism teaches anything, it tends to support the doctrine that the rapture occurs as a separate event from Christ's return to the earth to reign.

The entire figure casts in beautiful ideology the whole work of Christ for the church. From Christ's love for His own, He gave Himself for her on the Cross. The present age is one of preparation and sanctification of the bride. The ultimate goal is that the bride may be presented as stated in Ephesians 5:27 as "a glorious church, not having spot, or wrinkle, or any such thing; but that it should be holy and without blemish." The glorious transformation of the church is in keeping with her heavenly destiny and is a triumph of the grace of God. That which formerly was ugly with sin, spiritually dead, and hopelessly under the wrath of God, is now transformed to reflect the very perfections of God Himself in that it is a glorious church. All evidence of its previous lost condition is wiped away, and the church stands complete and perfect as a trophy of the grace of God. This is in keeping with God's purpose as stated in Ephesians 2:7, that the church "in the ages to come" might reflect "the exceeding riches of His grace and His kindness toward us through Christ Jesus." The church is going to be the major demonstration of the grace of God. Although saints of other ages are also saved by grace, apparently the church is singled out to demonstrate this particular facet of the infinite perfections of God's person and work. The total program of God in salvation is, therefore, seen to be motivated by the love of God, and its consummation is the fulfillment and satisfaction of that love.

The Judgment Seat of Christ: New Privileges

The second and very important phase of God's future program for the church involves the new privileges that will be given to saints as a result of the judgment at the judgment seat of Christ. Frequently in the New Testament Christians are reminded that they will be judged by Christ at His coming and on that occasion be rewarded. The major passage is found in II Corinthians 5:8-11, "We are confident, I say, and willing rather to be absent from the body, and to be present with the Lord. Wherefore we labour, that, whether present or absent, we may be accepted of him. For we must all appear before the judgment seat of Christ; that every one may receive the things done in his body, according to that he hath done, whether it be good or bad."

As Paul labored in the gospel, he was constantly aware of the fact that ultimately he would have to give an account to the Lord. What was true of him was true of all believers who would appear before the judgment seat of Christ. It is clear from this passage that the judgment concerns Christians only, as defined by the word "we." The judgment seat of Christ is, therefore, an event different from many other judgments, such as the judgment of the nations (MATTHEW 25), the judgment of Israel (EZEKIEL 20), or the great white throne judgment (REVELATION 20). This is an event which occurs immediately after the rapture and before Christ's second coming to establish His earthly Kingdom. The purpose of the judgment is not to ascertain the salvation of those involved; this has been already determined by the very fact that they are present, having been resurrected or translated. The issue is that of reward or recognition of faithful service.

In the New Testament three figures are used to illustrate the character of this judgment. In Romans 14:10-12 this judgment is likened to a steward giving account. Paul writes, "But why dost thou judge thy brother? or why dost thou set at nought thy brother? for we shall all stand before the judgment seat of Christ. For it is written, As I live, saith the Lord, every knee shall bow to me, and every tongue shall confess to God. So then every one of us shall give account of himself to God." The exhortation is addressed to each individual to judge himself rather than others, because "every one of us shall give account of himself to God." A steward, by nature of his office and responsibilities, is one to whom are committed the goods of another. Everything a Christian has, whether it be salvation, health, money, privilege, natural or spiritual gifts, is all sovereignly bestowed by God. Of these every Christian is a steward. At the judgment seat of Christ, accordingly, an account will be given of our stewardship. Our primary concern, therefore, should not be to judge others, often by comparison to our own supposed superiority. Rather, we should concentrate on our own lives and seek to fulfill our stewardship faithfully in view of this future time of reckoning.

The concept of a steward is at once challenging and reassuring. A steward is not responsible for goods which have not been committed to him. Too often Christians have a sense of guilt because they have not performed works and do not have gifts which properly belong to another. At the judgment seat of Christ the only question will be what we have done with what God has committed to *us*. A person with comparatively few talents and opportunities will be judged on the basis of those he has, while the person with many gifts and opportunities will be judged accordingly. The issue as stated in I Corinthians 4:2 is the question of how faithful we have been: "Moreover it is required in stewards, that a man be found faithful." Unquestionably, at the judgment seat of Christ there will be many surprises. Christians who live in comparative obscurity with no apparent great talent or service for God may be judged more faithful than those in prominent places who have had great opportunities, but only partially entered into them. This doctrine should be a great comfort to every Christian, especially those laboring in difficult circumstances which limit their money, strength, and natural and spiritual gifts. The ultimate question is not how successful or how public our good works are, but rather how faithful we have been in the appointed task.

A second major illustration is to be found in I Corinthians 3:11-15, where a Christian's life is compared to a building:

"For other foundation can no man lay than that is laid, which is Jesus Christ. Now if any man build upon this foundation gold, silver, precious stones, wood, hay, stubble; every man's work shall be made manifest: for the day shall declare it, because it shall be revealed by fire; and the fire shall try every man's work of what sort it is. If any man's work abide which he hath built thereupon, he shall receive a reward. If any man's work shall be burned, he shall suffer loss: but he himself shall be saved; yet so as by fire."

In this figure the foundation is supplied—namely, that which Christ Himself has given us both by way of salvation and provision for our life. On this foundation, supplied of God, the individual believer as well as the church corporately should build. Six materials are mentioned: gold, silver, precious stones, wood, hay, or stubble. Although the passage does not expound on these materials, it is obvious that they have symbolic meaning. Gold perhaps refers to that which glorifies God. Silver, the metal of redemption, may indicate evangelism and soul-winning. The precious stones may represent all the many good works which Christians can perform. By contrast, wood, hay, and stubble represent three degrees of worthlessness: wood, that which is good for a time but not eternity; hay, that which is good for animals but not for man; and stubble, that which is comparatively worthless.

Paul declares that the building shall be tested by fire: "The fire shall try every man's work of what sort it is." The important question is what will remain after the searching fire of God's judgment. The gold, silver, and precious stones will remain after the fire has burned the combustible materials, and will be the basis for reward. The Apostle makes plain, however, that the issue is not salvation, for he states in the concluding passage, "If any man's work shall be burned, he shall suffer loss: but he himself shall be saved; yet so as by fire." He gives a further word of comfort in I Corinthians 4:5, where he states in connection with this judgment, "Then shall every man have praise of God." Apparently, every believer will have some ground for at least partial reward.

Questions have often been raised as to the exact character of this judgment. What reward can be given to a Christian who is already perfect in Christ and who has everything in his relationship to the Lord? Part of the answer is given in other Scriptures, which speak of various crowns which Christians will receive at the judgment seat of Christ. In II Corinthians 4:8 mention is made of the crown of righteousness, which is a recognition of a holy life. In

James 1:12 and Revelation 2:10 eternal life itself is spoken of as a crown. In I Peter 5:4 a crown of glory is mentioned, and in I Corinthians 9:25 reference is made to the incorruptible crown.

In connection with the mention of the incorruptible crown a third figure is introduced, namely, the figure of a race (1 CORIN-THIANS 9:24-27). Here the Apostle challenges the Corinthians, "Know ye not that they which run in a race run all, but one receiveth the prize? So run, that ye may obtain." He goes on to point out how an athlete running a race must be self-controlled or temperate. Everything must be put aside in order to win. He declares in I Corinthians 9:26, "I therefore so run, not as uncertainly; so fight I, not as one that beateth the air." He instead exerts every effort and exercises control, as he stated in I Corinthians 9:27: "But I keep under my body, and bring it into subjection: lest that by any means, when I have preached to others, I myself should be a castaway [disapproved]." As a runner in a race must not take time to look back to see whether other runners may be overtaking him, and must disregard the cheering grandstands and the natural inclination to rest and slow down, so the Christian must strive to the end that he may obtain a crown.

In running the race the runner must not only discipline his own body, but he must keep the rules of the game. He must keep his body in subjection lest he be disapproved or disqualified from the reward. As in a modern athletic contest where a runner must not start ahead of the "go" gun or stray off the prescribed path, so the Christian must operate according to the divine rules if he is to win the prize. His priorities must put God first and all else second. The winner in the race will get more than the corruptible crown, a crown of laurel leaves which normally was given Greek athletes who won a contest; he will win an incorruptible crown, namely, a reward that will continue forever.

The various crowns which believers will receive are, of course, all the result of the wonderful grace of God. Those who receive their rewards will freely acknowledge that the glory belongs to Christ. In keeping with this, the four and twenty elders of Revelation 4:10 cast their crowns before the throne. If this representative company is the church in heaven, clearly the judgment seat of Christ will be no place of boasting, but all from the least to the greatest will acknowledge that apart from the grace of God they would have been undone as lost sinners.

The question has been raised as to the precise nature of the resulting reward. What will be the practical outcome of the judgment seat of Christ? II Corinthians 5 states simply "that every one may receive the things done in his body, according to that he hath done, whether it be good or bad." II Corinthians 5:11 goes on to speak of the "terror of the Lord."

It seems clear from other Scriptures that the judgment seat of Christ is not a place where the believer is condemned. When Christ died for the sins of believers, obviously He died for all our sins. The believer, therefore, is justified by faith (ROMANS 5:1), and there is "now no condemnation to them which are in Christ Jesus" (ROMANS 8:1). This is again expressed in John 3:18: "He that believeth on him is not condemned," and in John 5:24 Christ said, "Verily, verily, I say unto you, He that heareth my word, and believeth on him that sent me, hath everlasting life, and shall not come into condemnation; but is passed from death unto life."

It is clear that in our present experience it is necessary for believers to confess their sins. According to I John 1:9, "If we confess our sins, he is faithful and just to forgive us our sins, and to cleanse us from all unrighteousness." This forgiveness, however, is not judicial forgiveness, but resembles the family relationship of a father to a son, and has to do with present sanctification, present fellowship, and present fruitfulness.

Some have tried to infer from the language of the judgment seat of Christ that it constitutes a purgatory for sins not previously confessed, and a time of weeping and regret for those who have not served Christ suitably. No one should minimize the solemnity of this important occasion, referred to by Paul in the expression "the terror of the Lord." However, what Paul feared was not divine judgment, but the condemnation of his own heart as he contemplated the review that would take place at that time of all that he had done for Christ. At the judgment seat of Christ no chastening, such as is sometimes experienced in our present life, would be suitable. At that judgment the believer is already holy as Christ is holy, and has a new nature in which there is no sin principle operating. Of what use would a disciplinary judgment be in such a situation? The Scriptures themselves describe the difference not in judgment but as a matter of reward, and the rewards will differ according to what a man has done for Christ.

The question of course still remains: What are these rewards?

If we cast our crowns at Christ's feet and recognize it is all of the grace of God, in what sense is one Christian going to be different from another at the judgment seat of Christ?

The answer to this difficult question seems to be that rewards will differ in the sense that Christians in heaven will be given different aspects of privileged service for Christ. It is clear that in eternity Christians will not be idle, but will have places of ministry as "his servants" (REVELATION 22:3). This is also illustrated in the account of the pounds in Luke 19:11-27, although this passage has its primary application to the millennial kingdom. The principle is laid down that those who are faithful will be given larger spheres of service. Hence, in eternity the rewards Christians will receive for faithful service here will be in the form of privileged places of service in Christ's eternal kingdom. Just as the members of athletic teams in our colleges are chosen on the basis of their showing in practice, so in heaven Christians who have been faithful in their time of testing on earth will be allotted places of service accordingly in the eternal state. These rewards will be much like a diploma at graduation exercises in any school. Although students may differ in their academic achievements and some graduate with more honor than others, all receive recognition for what they have done. Graduation is a time of reward, not of punishment, and although some students may regret that they have not done better, the emphasis seems to be on the happy note of achievement.

In view of the confrontation, however, which all believers will have at the judgment seat of Christ, the admonition of Paul concerning "the terror of the Lord," that is, the godly fear that he will fall short, should guide Christians into paths of faithfulness and to judge the issues of life with a system of priorities which will put eternal things first.

The New Dwelling Place: The New Jerusalem

Christians in heaven, however, will not only rejoice in new bodies patterned after the body of Christ, a new relationship of marriage to the heavenly bridegroom, and new privileges in service, but the church also will have a new dwelling place. Whereas their state in general is to be "with Christ," their ultimate destiny in the eternal state is the New Jerusalem.

It is clear that at the time of the rapture Christians are caught up and taken to the Father's house, namely, heaven or the Presence of God. According to the premillennial interpretation of Scripture, saints accompanied by the holy angels will proceed in procession from heaven to the earth on the occasion of the second coming of Christ (REVELATION 19:11-21). After the millennium, however, their ultimate dwelling place is in the New Jerusalem on the new heaven and earth which will succeed the present creation. The description given in Revelation 21-22 pictures in symbolic language a beautiful city descending from heaven to the earth. The implication is that the New Jerusalem has been in existence prior to this event, and may be a reference to the prepared place mentioned in John 14:2-3. Some believe that it will be a satellite city over the earth during the millennium, and the home of resurrected and translated saints during the thousand-year reign of Christ. In any event, in Revelation 21 the New Jerusalem is pictured as descending from heaven to the new earth. Scholars are not agreed on the extent to which this passage should be interpreted literally, but inasmuch as obviously the saints will need a place in which to dwell in eternity, until we have reason to question it the best interpretation is to regard it as an actual city having the appearance and characteristics that are herein described.

According to Revelation 21 the city is foursquare, 12,000 furlongs or 1,342 miles on each side. It has the same height as it has width and length, and may be in the form of a cube or a pyramid. The city is characterized by translucent materials adorned with many precious jewels, and the light and glory are in keeping with the presence of God in the city. All that is evil is excluded, and the saints of all nations—whether Jews, Gentiles, or the church, the body of Christ—find their entrance into this eternal city. Although many questions remain unanswered, the passage makes clear that the ultimate state of those in Christ is one of complete blessing, of unending joy and peace, and of the wonderful spiritual fellowship that will exist between Christ and those who put their trust in him.

All of those wonderful events await the coming of the bridegroom for the bride, which will begin the series of prophetic fulfillments anticipated in the prophetic Word. Surely Christians, living in an age where there is so much that seemingly contradicts God's government and righteousness, can look forward in longing to this future prospect assured to all who put their trust in Jesus Christ as Saviour and Lord. With John, the Christian today can breathe the prayer, "Even so, come, Lord Jesus" (REVELATION 22:20).